# LOST SANDUSKY

# LOST SANDUSKY

M. KRISTINA SMITH

THE History PRESS

Published by The History Press
Charleston, SC 29403
www.historypress.net



First published 2015

Manufactured in the United States

ISBN 978.1.62619.586.8

Library of Congress Control Number: 2015935122

*This book is dedicated in loving memory of my grandmother, Martha Meister.*

# CONTENTS

# ACKNOWLEDGEMENTS

There are many people whose help and support made this book possible, and I want to thank them. Researching the history of so many different topics can sometimes be a daunting task, and many people helped point me in the right direction or assisted me with the research.

I would like to thank the staff of the Rutherford B. Hayes Presidential Center, especially Nan Card and Gil Gonzalez; the staff of the Sandusky Library, especially Ron Davidson; and the staff at the Ottawa County Historical Museum. Ohio is fortunate to have these institutions with fantastic historical archives and knowledgeable and extremely helpful staffs. All of you were hugely supportive and kind, and I am so very grateful to you.

Thank you to fellow author Glenn C. Kuebeler, who was a huge help in sharing his knowledge and some of his records, pointing me in the right direction for some of my research and being very supportive of this project. I also want to thank Bryan Edwards, Cedar Point public relations manager, for helping with the Cedar Point chapters.

The late historian Charles Frohman's work also was a big help in my research in that he amassed a huge collection of historical photos and documents from the region that he donated to the Hayes Center; he even indexed topics of interest in the Sandusky newspapers that are archived on microfilm. This was a great resource for researching Sandusky's past.

I want to thank my parents, Al and Faith Smith, who helped with some of the research for this book and helped with editing. Thank you to Jonathon

# ACKNOWLEDGEMENTS

Bird for taking some of the photos for this book and converting many of the photos into a suitable format for print.

Thank you to the many people who let me interview them for this book. I enjoyed meeting all of you and hearing your stories, and I appreciate your willingness to help and your enthusiasm for the book.

And thank you to The History Press for commissioning this book and to my editor, Greg Dumais, for all of your help and support.

There are numerous people I want to thank for their encouragement throughout this project, especially John Popson; my sister, Jennifer Smith-Margraf; my brother-in-law, Joe Margraf; my extended family; my friends; and my coworkers at the Fremont *News-Messenger* and *Port Clinton News Herald*. Your support and belief in this project meant so much to me.

I greatly enjoyed researching this book and learning more about a truly special community.

# INTRODUCTION

Sandusky, Ohio, has been known as the "Color Capital of the World," "Ice Capital of the Great Lakes" and "America's Roller Coast."

At one time, it was the largest freshwater fish market in the world and was the biggest producer of ice west of the Hudson River.

Everything from boats to crayons to wine has been manufactured here.

It was a port for travelers passing through on steamboats or one of several railroad lines. One of these travelers was English author Charles Dickens, who stayed at one of the hotels for a night.

Sandusky was a major stop on the Underground Railroad, with places all over town slaves hid before crossing the lake to freedom in Canada.

The city itself is laid out in an unusual pattern. The downtown streets form the symbol of the Freemasons. The man who laid out Sandusky, Hector Kilbourne, was the grand master of the first Masonic Lodge here.

Sandusky has a rich and varied history.

In the days of American Indians and pioneer settlers, Sandusky was considered a rich area for the fur trade and later would be a strategically important location for military forces during the French and Indian War and the War of 1812.

Sandusky was settled, in part, because of the Revolutionary War. The city is part of a region called the Firelands. During the Revolutionary War, the British set fire to towns in Connecticut, and residents lost their homes in the flames. To compensate them, Connecticut gave them land in the Firelands, which is the western portion of the

Western Reserve, property Connecticut owned that stretched across northeast Ohio.

Sandusky was first called Ogontz Place, named for an Ottawa Indian chief. It consisted of a cabin and a trading post. Then, in 1817, Zalmon Wildman laid out a village that he called Portland in part of what is today Sandusky. Another man, Isaac Mills, made a claim on land that was in Wildman's territory. The pair made a compromise and joined their land to make a city, which they named Sandusky. Sandusky meant "at the cold water" in one of the American Indian languages, according to Hewson L. Peeke's *A Standard History of Erie County Vol. 1*. In 1818, Kilbourne platted the city, and the streets today still form the Masonic symbol.

Industry quickly sprang up. Anglers discovered the Sandusky Bay was rich with fish, and they caught and sold everything from walleye—then more commonly called pickerel—to sturgeon.

More settlers came, some stopping in the area on their way out west and others choosing to stay. A pioneer in public transportation, Sandusky was the site of Ohio's first railroad.

Cedar Point drew swimmers and later began being developed as an amusement park. It quickly became a huge draw, as it remains today with some of the tallest and fastest roller coasters in the world.

Although some things remain the same, much has changed in Sandusky over the years. Historic buildings and industries have come and gone. With them are memories that would be lost to history were it not for the historians, local people and newspapers that documented them.

This book details some of those fascinating places that are part of "Lost Sandusky."

# 1
# WHERE WAS FORT SANDUSKY?

Decades before the United States was a country, the French, American Indians and English fought territorial battles—including the seven-year French and Indian War for control of the Ohio country and other Great Lakes regions.

The Ohio country was strategically and naturally desirable, according to Paul Moon, president of the Ottawa County Historical Society. Lake Erie and the Ohio River were gateways to traveling farther west, and they provided an abundance of fresh water. The Ohio country also was 90 percent forested and filled with animals that could be trapped for the fur trade, Moon said.

"It was the first available land west of the Alleghenies, which were already settled," he said, referring to the Allegheny Mountains. "It was contested by the Indians because that's where they lived."

The Sandusky Bay, known then as "Lake Sandusky" or even "Lake St. Dusky," became a tactical area in their disputes. Through the 1700s, the French and the British built forts along the bay. Both gave some of these forts the name Fort Sandusky, although historians have found different spellings, including Sandoksi and Sandoske.

There was actually more than one Fort Sandusky. For more than a century, historians have disputed how many Forts Sandusky actually existed, who used them and where they were. Travel to Port Clinton, and you'll find a marker at the end of Fulton Street on the bay side noting that Fort Sandusky stood there. But head east to Sandusky to the spot that once was the village of Venice, and you'll also find a marker for Fort Sandusky there.

Through the years, historians have learned that both markers are probably correct because there were a few forts in the area, and at least two of them were called Fort Sandusky, according to the late Charles Frohman, a Sandusky historian who amassed a huge collection of records and photos that he donated to the Rutherford B. Hayes Presidential Center. The Fort Sandusky near Port Clinton might actually have been farther out on the bay than believed and now covered by the water, as conditions have changed in the past 250 years, according to Frohman's writings on file at the Hayes Center.

"How far out in the bay the site of the fort is now cannot accurately be determined, perhaps about 2 miles," Hewson L. Peeke wrote in his book *The Centennial History of Erie County, Ohio, Vol. 1*, published in 1925.

The men who traveled the area—and in some cases helped build one of the forts—shed some light on which was which and where each was, thanks to the journals they kept of their travels and activities.

Most historians and history enthusiasts who wrote papers and books on file at the Hayes Center and Ottawa County Historical Museum agree on this: in 1745, a Huron chief named Nicolas—whose given name was Orontony but was changed at his baptism—lived in the Sandusky area. He was allied with the French and had a fort on the Sandusky Bay. The chief became unhappy with the French for unknown reasons and allied himself with the English. When the French found out, the chief abandoned his plans, burned down the fort and left the area.

There are different versions of the details. Some believe Nicolas's fort, which may have been a simple blockhouse, was at Port Clinton, on the north side of the bay. Frohman wrote in his records that the location of the fort was never determined.

Others contend that the French built the fort that Nicolas manned. And still other accounts say that Nicolas befriended English traders and allowed them to build the fort.

"English traders first made their appearance in the Ohio country in 1699–1700," according to the book *Old Fort Sandoski of 1745 and the Sandusky Country* by Lucy Elliot Keller, who cited an 1871 writing by A.T. Goodman, secretary of the Western Reserve Historical Society. "From that time until 1745, we frequently hear of them in various towns and stations. In 1745, they built a small fort or blockhouse among the Hurons on the north side of Sandusky Bay.

"In 1748, they were driven off by a party of French soldiers from Detroit."

An early map often referenced in many accounts says the fort at Port Clinton was "usurped by the French in 1751." Historians have referred to this Fort Sandusky as the first fort in Ohio built by white settlers, according to *Old Fort Sandoski of 1745 and the Sandusky Country*, which was published by the Ohio Historical Society, and Peeke's *The Centennial History of Erie County, Ohio, Vol. 1*.

The journals of French engineer and soldier Joseph Gaspard Chaussegros de Léry of Quebec, discovered in 1906 at a university in Montreal, helped answer some questions about the fort, according to *Old Fort Sandoski*. He specifically refers to a French fort on the Sandusky Bay.

In 1754, de Léry was on an expedition from Erie, Pennsylvania, to Detroit. That August, he noted finding the ruins of the fort "Sandoske on Lac Sandoske" about two miles from what is now Port Clinton. He referred to the fort as being French.

"I imagined that some vestiges still remained of the fort the French had built in 1751 and which was afterwards evacuated," he wrote on August 4, according to the book. "To find it, I followed the shore on the north side of the said lake which runs East and West.

"After proceeding about 3 leagues [about nine nautical miles], I found a clearing where I landed at noon and discovered the ruins of the old fort."

In de Léry's journals, he also mentions the portage, the land route over which travelers could carry their canoes to avoid rowing around the Marblehead Peninsula, a longer and more dangerous route. The portage ran across what today is Fulton Street, from the bay side to where it ends at Lake Erie near the mouth of the Portage River. The Portage River sometimes was called the Carrying River in historical records, and it further illustrates the importance of this route.

The portage, which likely added to the fort's strategic value, is sometimes called the de Léry Portage and is frequently mentioned in historical records.

About sixty years after de Léry passed through, the forts were gone, but the portage would play an important role in the War of 1812. General William Henry Harrison used it to bring cannons and arms in canoes for his men, who assembled at the Lake Erie side of Fulton Street while preparing to invade Canada in 1813, Moon said.

"It's an astounding place," Moon said of the portage.

The French and Indian War officially began in 1756 and was fought over territorial disputes between the French and English. This is where the English Fort Sandusky in Venice enters the story.

In September 1760, the French surrendered their American holdings, and the English sent out soldiers to take possession of French forts. On the way, they destroyed another fort on the bay, Fort Jundat in some records—which was believed to be on Pickerel Creek near present-day Fremont, according to *Old Fort Sandoski*.

As the British passed through the area, they again realized the strategic importance of having a fort on the Sandusky Bay between trading posts and other forts.

"A small post at Sandusky would be useful for communication with Pittsburg [*sic*]," Captain Campbell of Detroit wrote to another officer in December 1760, according to the Ohio Historical Society's book.

By August, the British had issued orders to construct a fort there, and a month later, Lieutenant Elias Meyer was surveying the area with a plan to build. The fort, built at Venice, was done by February 1761 because correspondence between officers shows that "Lieutenant Meyer has left Ensign Pauli and fifteen men at Sandusky," Keeler wrote.

Pauli was left in charge of the fort, and he was growing concerned that the American Indians in the area, who were not pleased the fort was there, might cause problems, according to a February 1762 letter he sent to a superior. By May, things had calmed down, but peace would not remain for long.

Chief Pontiac, an Ottawa tribe leader born in what is present-day Ohio, did not want to live under British rule, so he united multiple tribes to fight off the British. His plan was to attack English forts in the Great Lakes region on the same day. That day came on May 16, 1763. Nine English forts were captured during what is called Pontiac's Conspiracy, and one of them was Fort Sandusky.

The day started innocently for Pauli, who was told that a group of natives wanted to speak with him. He let them in, and the group smoked pipes and began to talk. Then one of them raised his hand in a signal, and the astonished Pauli was disarmed while gunfire broke out in the fort. He was taken prisoner and left the fort to see his garrison lying dead, Keeler wrote.

The natives took him prisoner, and as they walked him to their canoes, he saw Fort Sandusky engulfed in flames. The American Indians took him back to Detroit. He expected to be burned alive, but instead, the group threw stones at him and made him sing and dance.

They then plunged him into water to symbolically remove the white blood from his veins and forced him to marry an American Indian widow. Pauli later escaped and found refuge at Fort Detroit, according to *Old Fort Sandoski*.

Yet this was not the end of the forts named Sandusky. A little more than a year after Fort Sandusky was destroyed in Pontiac's Conspiracy, the British decided to build another fort on the Sandusky Bay.

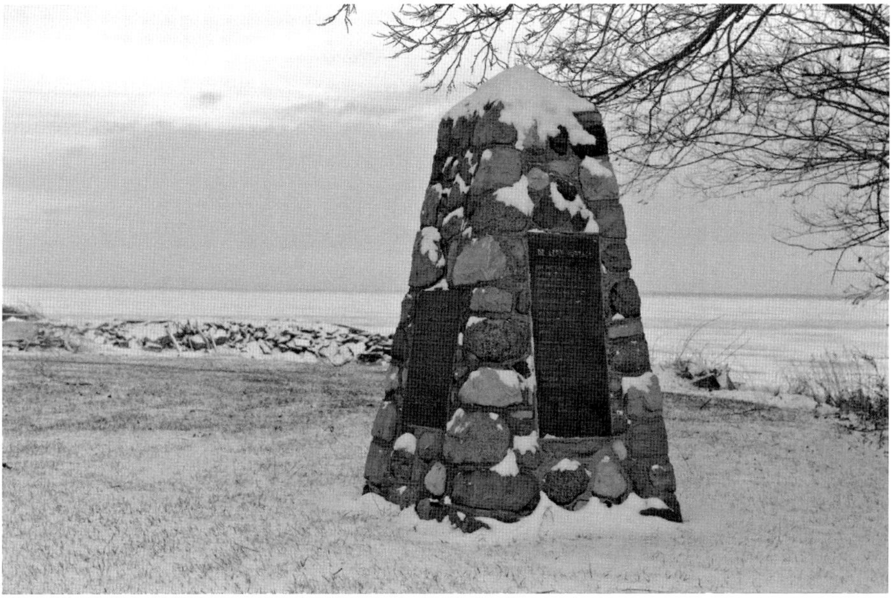

The monument for Fort Sandusky in Port Clinton initially had an incorrect inscription and was later changed. *Photo by Jonathon Bird.*

English engineer John Montressor also kept a journal in 1764, and he noted receiving orders to build another fort where "Old Sandoski" stood. Construction on the fort, which was to be located about three-quarters of a mile from the old French Fort Sandusky, was underway in September 1764, but it was abandoned after the British learned the American Indians were planning an attack. On October 18, the "whole decamped and embarked for Niagara," Keeler wrote.

So ended the last Fort Sandusky.

A dispute over whether the forts were all located in Port Clinton continued into the twentieth century. In 1912, various historical and local organizations joined to erect the monument on Fulton Street in Port Clinton. The original inscription said all of the Forts Sandusky, including the one burned down in Pontiac's Conspiracy, were located at the same area in Port Clinton.

That inscription was wrong, historians said. Paper after paper on file at the Ottawa County Historical Museum and the Rutherford B. Hayes Presidential Center explains that the forts could not all have been in the same location. The writers pointed out that the English fort at Venice is mentioned several times in Erie County records, including an 1831 survey of Margaretta Township, which includes Venice.

Their arguments and research ultimately helped show that both areas likely were home to a Fort Sandusky. In 1965, the Ohio Historical Society put a new plaque at the Fulton Street monument in Port Clinton that no longer claims it was the site of the British fort burned in Pontiac's Conspiracy.

# 2
# VILLAGE OF VENICE

When Sandusky had one log cabin and was known mostly to American Indians, the village of Venice sprang up just west of Sandusky along the bay and quickly became the largest settlement west of Cleveland.

Venice was laid out in 1816–17 by War of 1812 veteran Major Frederick Falley, a Massachusetts native who had bought the land that would become the village and the surrounding land known as Margaretta Township.

Several hundred people from the East and South moved in and helped build two warehouses, various stores and homes in the area where Cold Creek meets the Sandusky Bay, according to the *Fire Lands Pioneer* September 1860 edition, a magazine published by the Firelands Historical Society in Norwalk at that time.

The first gristmill had been built along Cold Creek before the village was established, and others followed after settlers moved in. The first lumber sawmill was completed in 1815, according to Hewson L. Peeke's *A Standard History of Erie County Vol. 1*.

Venice had an advantage in the milling business because the mills were on Cold Creek, a stream fed by underground springs that maintains a constant temperature of forty-eight to fifty degrees. That constant temperature kept the creek from freezing in the winter, allowing mills to operate all year while those located elsewhere shuttered for the season, according to the *Lakefront News*.

Flour was Venice's big export, and it was an important product for pioneers. Flour from the village was sent to New York City and to Chicago, where it was sold to settlers moving west.

One of the larger mills, built by pioneer Russell Heywood, opened in 1831 and ran almost constantly to meet demand. Heywood also built another mill in the nearby Castalia area. Gertrude M. Chapman, who grew up in Venice, remembered seeing three hundred men working at one time in a village flour mill—she didn't specify which one—to keep up with demand, according to her historical account of Venice in Peeke's book. Chapman grew up in Venice and was eighty-four when Peeke's book was published in 1916.

Steamboats pulled up to a pier built six hundred feet into the Sandusky Bay to load up the various goods made in Venice, said Glenn C. Kuebeler, author of the book *Castalia, Cold Creek, and the Blue Hole.*

Massachusetts native Judge H. Fowler first visited Venice in the winter of 1818 and deemed it a booming pioneer town.

"Considerable trade at the time was carried on; large quantities of salt were sold, not only to the people of the Firelands, but to cities of Richmond, Knox and other counties," Fowler wrote in the June 1867 edition of *Fire Lands Pioneer.*

That would change, and Sandusky eventually would develop its own industry and shipping port, ultimately overtaking Venice. Historical accounts give insight on some of the issues that led to Venice's demise.

During the summer of 1818, the village residents were struck with an epidemic of some sort of sickness, which killed some of the prominent residents, sickened many and caused some to leave, according to the *Pioneer.* This was a disaster for the village's progress.

Fowler, who moved to Venice a few months after his initial visit, lived through the sickness and cared for family members who were ailing, according to his account in the *Pioneer.*

He believed the illness came from the nearby marsh during the extreme heat of summer. Although the illness hasn't been given a specific name, historical accounts said those stricken suffered from fever and ague, which is a malarial fever with hot and cold sweating fits.

"In those days, fever and ague meant something," Fowler wrote.

> *It was most horrible to endure. I have seen "shakes" last two hours...after the shakes, the patient generally fell into a tranquil sleep for a short time, then came a high fever, delirium, all sorts of indistinct talking, a burning thirst that continued for hours; then the patient, as the fever subsided, became more quiet—perhaps would rest tolerably through the night—in the morning take some breakfast and have a short time to wait for the returning operation, which was repeated day after day, week after week, for an indefinite period.*

Every family had sickness, and many children died, Fowler wrote. The town's population dwindled, but it recovered as mills went up, according to the *Pioneer*.

This indicates that although illness might have hurt Venice for a few years, the village did rebound, at least for a while. The *Pioneer* noted Venice was known as an exporter of flour, and newspaper accounts show commerce continued there for decades after the sickness. Chapman also said in Peeke's book that disease was not a factor and that many places across the country had fever and ague.

"The decline of Venice was due to the shallowness of the water, which prevented large vessels from coming here," according to Chapman's account.

More information comes from William Watts Folwell, whose autobiography was published in 1933. Folwell had married Heywood's daughter, and the couple moved to Venice so Folwell could help with the mills. Heywood was living in Buffalo, New York, but maintained his business in the Venice area.

When Folwell, fresh from serving in the Civil War, arrived in Venice in July 1865, the small village consisted of two crossing streets. He kept the books and handled outgoing mail at the Heywood mill. He also was appointed the engineer on a project to build a macadam road from Sandusky through Venice and farther west.

By the 1860s, locals had learned that Venice, like the Lake Erie islands, was a fertile place for growing grapes for the wine industry. Some of Heywood's property was coveted for grape growing, and Folwell noted that he surveyed the property for Heywood. Folwell did not say in his book, however, whether the land was sold or whether grapes were grown there.

He passed the time by taking a small boat—the only one in Venice, he wrote—onto the Sandusky Bay. A German speaker, he made friends with German settlers, and he helped lead services at the Episcopalian church Heywood had built in the village. He also wrote columns for the *Sandusky Register* and was offered the editor job but turned it down.

"I was temperamentally adapted, I suppose, to the social life of the village, so far as any existed," Folwell wrote in his autobiography. "The only place of general evening assemblage was the schoolhouse. The store was the resort of men with anecdotes to tell, and there passed many a pleasant, leisurely hour during which I often listened while clerking.

"In all my time there, there was never a lecture, concert or play in Venice."

Still, the *Register* described Venice in 1867 as a pleasant hamlet with potential to grow, especially because of its three hundred acres of vineyards.

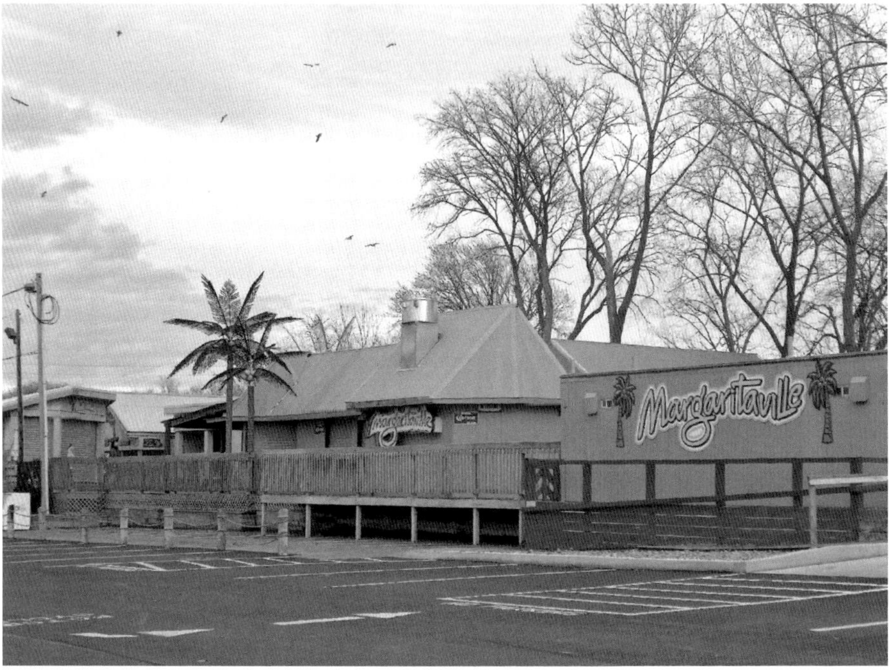


The Margaritaville restaurant was built on the remains of the Heywood mill in Venice. *Photo by Kristina Smith.*

"More vines are yearly being planted, and each season are coming into bearing; hence, the prediction of grapes may be regarded as rapidly increasing," the newspaper reported. "This increase, however, is not a spasmodic one, caused by excitement, but a healthy and steady growth that promises permanency and excellent results."

Folwell, who was never overly fond of the milling business, left Venice in 1868. He accepted a job as a professor at Kenyon College in Gambier, Ohio. He later would become the first president of the University of Minnesota.

The church Heywood built, which Folwell described as "charming," fell into disrepair after Heywood died in 1883. The members had either died or moved away, and there had never been a large number of people in the village to form a good-sized congregation, Folwell wrote.

"Not a vestige of the church remains, and I suppose there are few persons, perhaps none, who could now identify the site," according to Folwell's autobiography.

Heywood's Venice mill remained open until 1945. It was partially demolished, and its remains were turned into the Margaritaville restaurant on Ohio 6 along Cold Creek, Kuebeler said. The waterfall at the restaurant was the original waterfall made by the Heywood mill.

Venice remained a hamlet, and by the 1950s, Sandusky started taking steps to annex it into the city. A group of Venice residents tried to stop the move, but ultimately, the Ohio Supreme Court upheld the annexation.

Venice became part of Sandusky in 1963.

# 3
# BUSINESS AND INDUSTRY

## Ice Harvesting: An Industry Lost to Technology

When we want a glass of ice water, we usually go to the refrigerator and press one button for ice and one for water. We can pull nicely chilled ice cream from the freezer for a treat or thaw some frozen meat to put on the grill.

In the 1800s and early 1900s, things were not so convenient or simple. There were no refrigerators or ready-made ice cubes. People used iceboxes, wooden chests that kept food cool by using blocks of ice to cool the insulated compartments.

Ice came from Lake Erie, carefully cut and harvested each winter and stored for when it would be in demand. Years ago, Lake Erie routinely froze solid, something that doesn't happen every winter anymore.

Sandusky became the largest ice producer west of the Hudson River and was called the "Ice Capital of the Great Lakes" because of its "crystal blue, clear as glass," natural ice, according to the exhibit on harvesting at the Maritime Museum of Sandusky.

Seeing a good use for all that ice, enterprising people made a viable business from the solid lake and Sandusky Bay, where water tends to freeze first and becomes some of the thickest ice.

In 1886, Sandusky had twenty ice-harvesting businesses, not including companies that harvested ice for their own uses, such as commercial fishermen who would need it in the summer to keep their product fresh. Nearly fifty

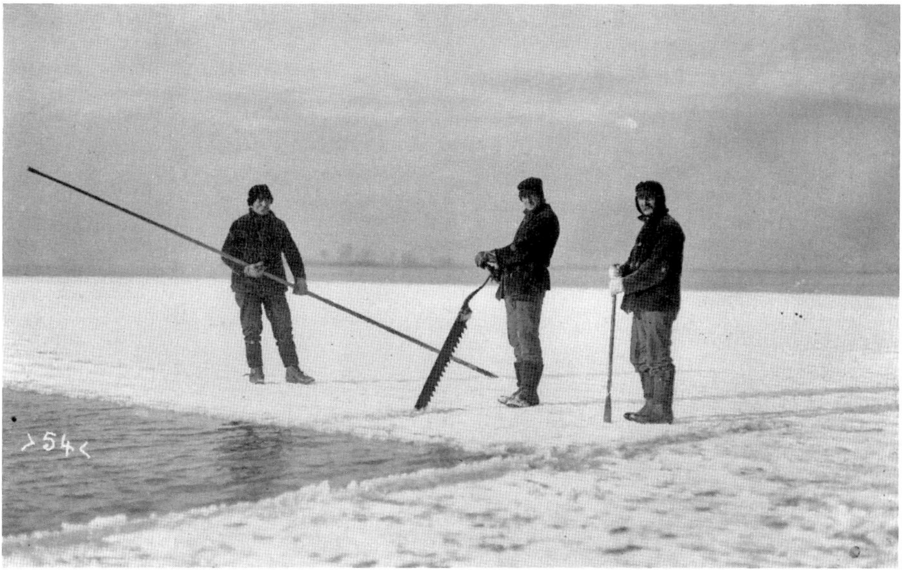

Men cut blocks of ice from Lake Erie's Sandusky Bay and saved them in icehouses. *Rutherford B. Hayes Presidential Center/Charles Frohman Collection.*

icehouses—buildings where ice was kept in sawdust, which was used as an insulator to keep it frozen—dotted the shoreline throughout Sandusky.

Getting the ice worked like this: Workers chose a field of ice and cut a two- to four-foot channel leading to a loading platform or icehouse. They would scrape the field clear of snow and mark off two-foot squares throughout the area. Then horses would pull ice plows that used chisel-like steel bars to cut the ice to a depth of five to seven inches.

Sawyers would cut through the blocks, and pickers would push them through the channel to the conveyers that would load the blocks onto trucks or send them directly to icehouses.

Workers would stack the blocks against one another and fill the cracks with sawdust and straw. In 1900, sawyers earned two dollars a day, and a day lasted ten hours.

By 1913, at least two thousand men worked in the ice-harvesting industry. That year, gas-powered saws made the sawyers' jobs easier.

The industry lasted until the early 1940s, when commercial refrigeration became widely available.

The last company to harvest ice in Sandusky was Lay Brothers, a commercial fishing business. In 1941, according to the museum, Lay Brothers pulled three thousand tons of ice from the lake for its operation.

## Lyman Boat Works

For more than a century, one of the most beloved brands of boats on the Great Lakes and beyond was made in Sandusky. Lyman Boat Works built a wooden boat that was stylish and rode smoothly through Lake Erie's notoriously rough waves.

The boats also were affordable, making them accessible to the middle class and adding to their reach and popularity. Although mass production of wooden Lymans ended in 1973, the Lyman models still have a large following among boat enthusiasts.

"They're great-looking boats," said Tom Koroknay, who restores Lymans through his business, Koroknay's Marine Woodworking in Lexington, Ohio. "What people love is the ride. They were designed for the short Lake Erie chop."

Koroknay bought the defunct company's tooling and archives in 1988 so that he could better make parts to restore his customers' boats and preserve the company's history. He also used the information to write a book on the history of the Lymans, called *Lyman Boats: Legend of the Lakes*. He said Lymans are some of the most popular wooden boats of all time.

Lymans got their start in 1873 in Cleveland when Bernard Lyman, an immigrant and cabinetmaker whose family came to the United States during the Civil War, made his first boat, a fifteen-foot wooden sailing skiff he used for fishing.

"It was out on loan so constantly that the young boat builder never had it available for himself," according to a January 1950 article in *Motor Boating* magazine. "He must have been a warm-hearted chap because he did not insist his friends moderate their demands so that he could once in a while use his own boat but solved the problem by building another.

"The second one was no sooner completed than it, too, was gone. So Bernard kept building—possibly with the slowly fading hope that one day he would have more than enough to satisfy all demands."

Then in 1875, Bernard and his brother, Ernst, founded Lyman Brothers Boat Builders of Cleveland, Ohio. The name would later be changed to Lyman Boat Works.

The brothers set up shop at the East Fortieth Street Livery in Cleveland and built skiffs and rowboats to meet demand at local liveries, according to Koroknay's book.

They used a method called lapstrake construction—also called clinker-built—to make the wooden creations, which were usually painted white.

With lapstrake, each wooden plank overlaps the next, and the planks are fastened by tack-style nails cinched over with steel block, according to Koroknay's book. The block is then bucked up on the inside of the hull, and nails are driven in from the outside.

The result was a durable yet stylish craft.

World War I was one of the reasons the company moved to Sandusky. The government needed the company's lakefront property for the war effort, so the Lymans started building boats at Bill Lyman's Cleveland home, according to Koroknay's book. Bill Lyman was Bernard's son, and by that time, he was in charge of the business.

After the war, Cleveland waterfront property was growing more expensive, and Lyman had built such a good name for itself that the Sandusky Chamber of Commerce tried to bring the company to its lakefront. The company agreed to the move and in 1928 started operations on First Street in Sandusky at Barr Rubber Products.

"We needed larger plant facilities than we had in Cleveland, but we also saw the advantages in Sandusky," Bill Lyman told the *Sandusky Register* on September 29, 1928. "The new site for our plant is close to Sandusky Bay, and this proximity to the water is a decided advantage for us in the matter of experimental work and also for demonstration purposes."

By then, Lyman Boat Works was making powerboats with outboard motors. Those boats were often raced on the Sandusky Bay, and participants could launch from the Lyman dock, according to Koroknay's book.

When the Great Depression started in 1929, Lyman changed its focus to cater to wealthier customers because the average person struggled for money just to buy food and had no cash for luxuries. Lyman also unveiled its Utility model, which became a mainstay of the business.

In 1938, Lyman Boat Works built its new factory on First Street near Barr Rubber, and its boat building quickly turned toward government boats during World War II. Lyman had several government contracts and built a utility boat, a flat-bottomed boat that could transport torpedoes and storm boats used to take GIs to beachheads, according to Koroknay's book. The company also collaborated on a wartime project with Matthews Boat Company in Port Clinton, which also made wooden boats.

Shortly after the war, wooden boats began their golden age. Lyman production peaked in 1955, when it made more than five thousand boats. By the mid-1950s, Lyman Boat Works was sending boats to more than two hundred dealers across the country.

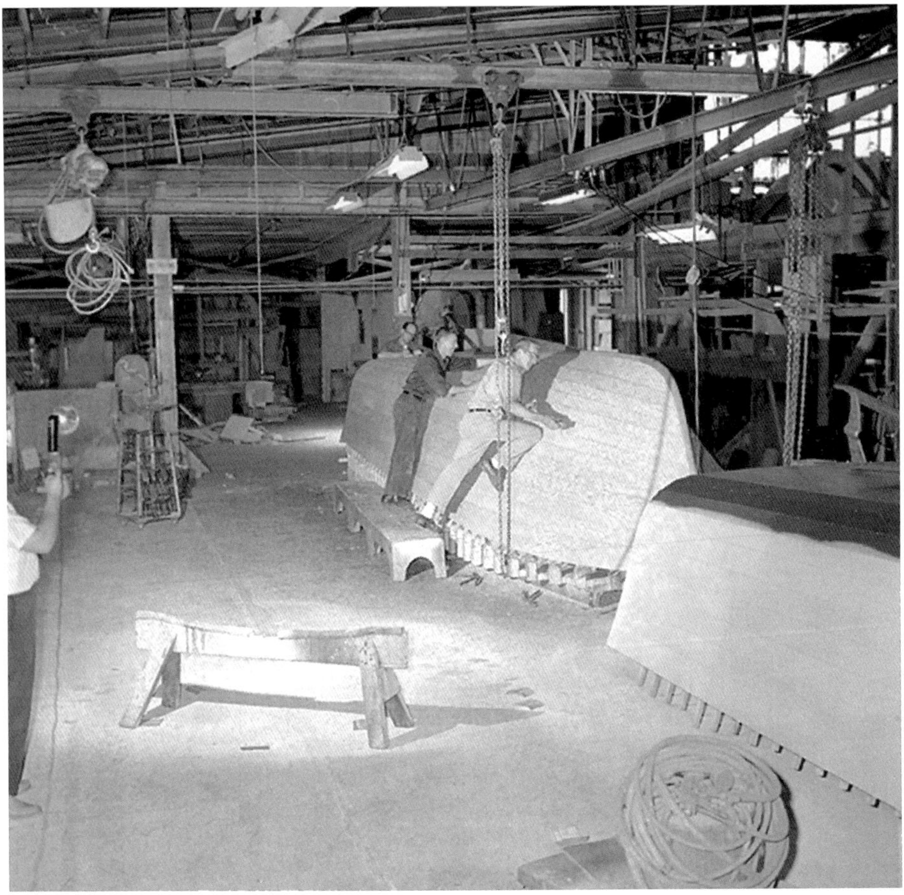

Lyman Boat Works employees craft one of the company's signature boats. *Photo courtesy of Tom Koroknay.*

After 1958, the business began its downfall. Bill Lyman died in 1953, and his widow, Hilda Lyman, and her son-in-law ran the business until Hilda Lyman retired in 1958, according to Koroknay's book.

The business then changed hands three more times. Labor disputes and corporate cuts hurt the company, and it fell behind its competitors, which began making fiberglass boats in the late '60s and early '70s, Koroknay said.

By 1974, plant workers were making about three hundred fiberglass boats a year, the *Register* reported that November.

"They just could never get off the ground with fiberglass, although the fiberglass boats were nice," Koroknay said.

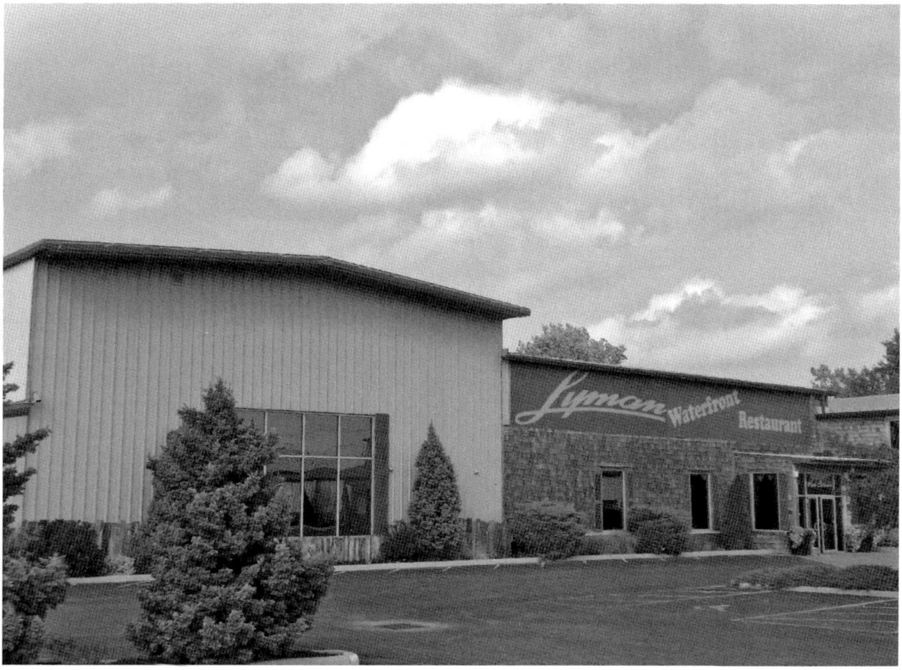


The Lyman factory was converted into a restaurant and event center. *Photo by Kristina Smith.*

Lyman Boat Works shut down in 1988 or 1989. From 1875 to 1973, the company had made more than sixty thousand wooden boats, according to Koroknay's book.

Today, the factory still stands and has been turned into a complex called Lyman Harbor. The complex has a waterfront restaurant, an area for weddings and other special events and a transient marina.

## American Crayon Company

To Sandusky Schools superintendent M.F. Cowdery, few sounds in the early 1800s were worse than chalk scratching a slate board.

At that time, chalk wasn't the substance we know today. It came to the United States by chance. Shippers used chalk from the cliffs of Dover, England, or Normandy, France, as ballast to balance their ships. When they reached the United States, they got rid of the chalk, often giving it to schools, according to the *Toledo Blade*.

The superintendent encouraged his brother-in-law, W.D. Curtis, to develop something better that didn't make an unsettling sound when pressed against the slate. In 1835, Curtis experimented with shipping chalk in the kitchen of his home and refined it into pure white crayon, which is more like the chalk used today, according to the *Cleveland Plain Dealer*. Back then, it was called crayon.

"Other schools heard about the pure white chalk and wanted it," the *Plain Dealer* reported. "A new American industry was born as a result."

This was also the beginning of the American Crayon Company, although it would not get that name until decades later. The company would become one of Sandusky's foremost industries and gave the city the moniker "Color Capital of the World."

Curtis established the Western School Supply Company to make and sell his chalk. He was not alone in the school supply industry. While Curtis was working in his kitchen, a dentist named Dr. Francis Field was doing similar work in the eastern United States and also developed a chalk that would not scratch slate, according to the *Sandusky Register*. The pair apparently did not know about each other's work. Field's work led to the Paramenter Crayon Company being founded in 1835 in Waltham, Massachusetts.

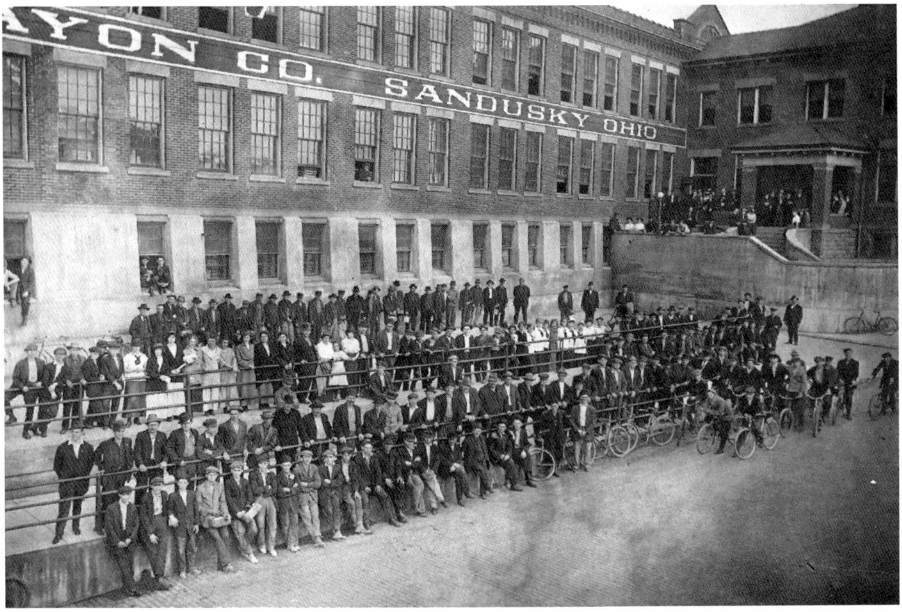


Employees from the American Crayon Company are pictured in this undated photo at the company's factory. *Sandusky Library Follett House Museum Archives.*

American Crayon Company formed in the 1890s when Western School Supply Company, Paramenter Crayon Company and Tiffin Crayon Company merged, according to the *Plain Dealer*.

The company would grow again and bring on another notable business, run by German immigrant Louis Prang of Boston, a photographer and printer. Prang got involved in the school supply business after he arrived in Boston and was shocked the school system didn't use color in the classroom, according to the *Blade*.

Prang introduced watercolor paints to the district, and it was the first in the United States to use color. He founded his own business, the Kroma Color Company, and imported colors from Germany to make watercolor paints, according to Sandusky Library Archives. Prang also is known as the father of the American Christmas card because he introduced the European tradition to America in 1875.

During World War I, Prang's color supply was shut down, so he turned to the American Crayon Company for colors. His company joined American Crayon Company in 1915, further expanding American Crayon's product line.

Through the decades, American Crayon thrived. It made school supplies like crayons, chalk, coloring books and watercolor paints and sent a magazine to teachers with craft ideas. But the products weren't limited to school art. The company made billiard and carpenter's chalk and crayons for textile mills and railroads, according to company brochures.

American Crayon Company also was the world's largest maker of small wooden boxes that were exclusively used in the Ford Model-T, the *Register* reported in 1988. The Model-T, which Ford made from 1908 to 1927, had a different ignition system than other cars. It had four coil boxes that were enclosed in a metal box mounted under a dashboard.

"The boxes had to be an exact size and were made of hard maple," according to the *Register*. "Henry Ford tried to find other companies to produce the boxes, but American Crayon was the only company that could meet the structural standards, and eventually all boxes were made in Sandusky."

The company changed hands in 1957, when the Joseph Dixon Crucible Company, which made graphite pencils, bought it. Then in the 1980s, another company merger changed the name to Dixon Ticonderoga.

The company's plant was located on Hayes Avenue at Columbus Avenue. It was built in 1874, burned down in 1901 and was immediately rebuilt, according to Sandusky Library Archives. Newspaper articles over the

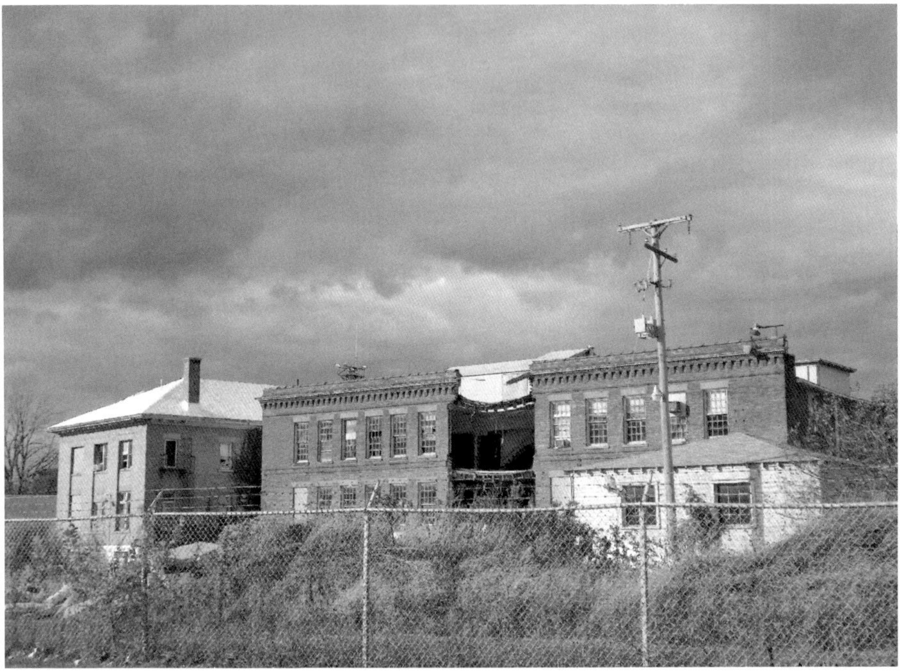

The American Crayon Company factory was in the process of being torn down in late 2014. *Photo by Kristina Smith.*

years show it employed more than two hundred people, and generations of the same families tended to work there. The company was the oldest manufacturer in Ohio, according to the *Blade*.

"There was a real closeness," former employee Chris Therkelsen told the *Register* in 1988. "Back then, when people started, they worked there for the rest of their lives."

American Crayon Company was a longtime source of pride for Sandusky. By the turn of the twenty-first century, Dixon Ticonderoga decided the plant was too old to compete with others that had already left the country, according to the *Blade*. The company laid off the local workers, moved the plant to Mexico and closed Sandusky operations in December 2002. Its departure was a huge blow to employees and the community.

"They worked through the Depression and everything," former employee Roger Bibler told the *Blade* of some of his fellow workers. "We never dreamed it would be gone just like that."

The plant was in the process of being demolished in 2015.

## Hinde and Dauch Paper Company

The company that revolutionized the paper packaging industry began in Sandusky when two local farm boys came up with new uses for straw that area farmers didn't need.

James J. Hinde and Jacob J. Dauch went into business together with a machine they took from farm to farm and used to thresh wheat and bale oats.

Their venture wasn't very profitable, though, and they usually had to wait until farmers sold crops to get paid, which was months after the pair actually did the work, according to the *Sandusky Register*. Instead of waiting, Hinde and Dauch took straw, a byproduct of the grain they thrashed, as payment. The pair then sold the straw to the Sandusky Paper Mill on Fillmore Street, which used it to make wrapping paper used by butchers.

In the late 1880s, Hinde and Dauch took over the struggling Sandusky Paper Mill and continued to make paper out of straw, according to newspaper articles and a company history on file at the Sandusky Library Archives. They incorporated their business, the Hinde and Dauch Paper Company, in 1900.

The pair thought straw paper would be a good cushion for shipping fragile products, and they began experimenting with new product ideas. Through their experiments, they developed a corrugated paper package called the Climax Wrapper. The wrapper was a piece of flat paper combined with corrugated paper that fit around a bottle for protection during shipping. It became wildly popular and was used to package everything from wine to medicine to pottery, the *Register* reported in 1905.

The wrapper would help Hinde and Dauch Paper Company become a pioneer in the modern packaging industry. The company also helped make Sandusky the cardboard capital of the world, according to the *Register*.

The Climax Wrapper was the company's main product in 1905, and it had "won high favor all over the world," the newspaper reported that year. It was considered the best wrapper of its kind on the market at that time, and the company sold the product across the United States and the world, according to the newspaper.

"The bottle wrapper revolutionized bottle shipping and helped increase the market and boost sales for some of its first users—winemakers in the Sandusky area," the *Register* reported.

But Hinde and Dauch continued experimenting with new ideas for the shipping industry. They developed a corrugated box by putting flat paper on both sides of the corrugated paper around 1906, according to a history

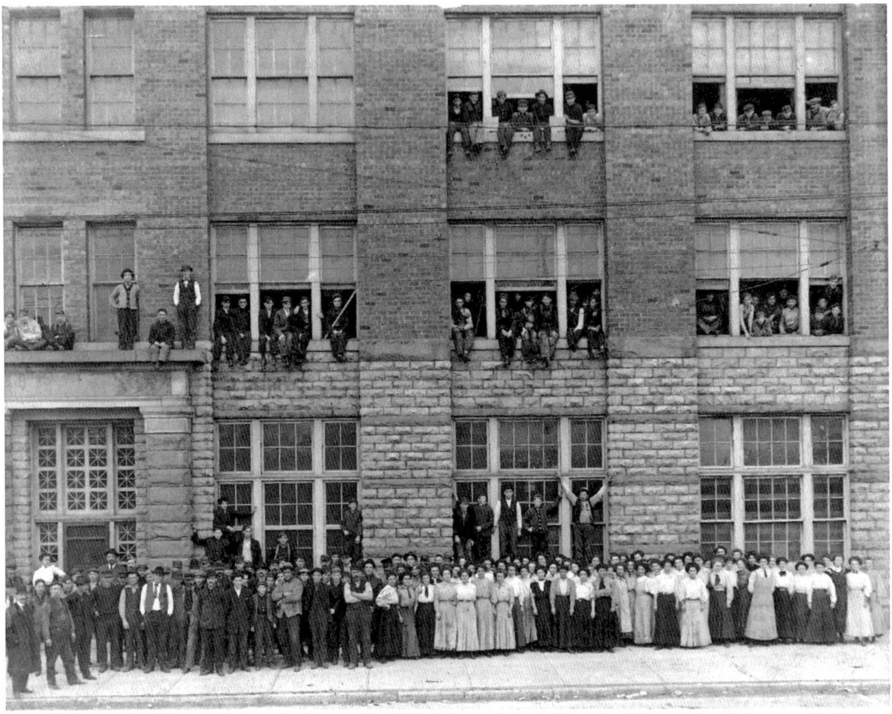

Hinde and Dauch employees pose for a photo at the company's factory at West Water and Decatur Streets. *Sandusky Library Follett House Museum Archives.*

of the company. This product was huge for the company and was quickly a favorite for shipping freight, especially by rail. The paper boxes were cheaper and lighter than the wooden crates often used at that time.

Although the company specialized in shipping products, it also made other items. The Acme bolster roll, for example, was a good seller. The roll was a long piece of cardboard with lace or fabric hanging from each end, and it was a decorative piece that was placed at the head of a bed, according to an ad from the March 1908 *Women's Endeavor* magazine. This "household necessity" could be shipped to any woman east of the Mississippi River for two dollars.

"An article for bed adornment—made of strong corrugated jute board—weighs only four pounds—there are various kinds—Acme is the best," the ad boasted.

In 1910, Hinde decided to pursue other business interests and sold his part of the company to Dauch. Hinde had helped found the Sandusky Automobile Manufacturing Company and also worked on developing farm tractors.

Business at Hinde and Dauch was still booming, and the company built a second straw paper mill that was finished the following year on Mills Street, according to the company history and *Register* articles. World War I added to production.

"The shortage of lumber for box making material, plus transportation needs to carry food stuffs and supplies to maintain our armies at home and at the front forced manufacturers in all lines to turn to the corrugated shipping box," according to the company history.

Over the years, the company had several mills and buildings for its manufacturing process, including a location in Norman Hall, which once was a performance venue on Water Street. Hinde and Dauch's flagship plant on Railroad Street (today Shoreline Drive) between Decatur and Jackson Streets and facing the Sandusky Bay was built in 1918. The company kept growing to meet demand for its shipping containers. The main Sandusky plant ultimately became the largest corrugated box plant in the world, according to the *Register*. Hinde and Dauch also built other plants in the United States and Canada.

Like Hinde, Dauch began pursuing tractor and car ventures, but he continued to own the paper company. One of his ventures was the Dauch Manufacturing Company, which was located on First Street and made gas-powered tractors, the *Register* reported. At the turn of the twentieth century, farmers still used horses and mules, so the gas-powered tractors were considered revolutionary. He also was president of the Eagle-Macomber Motor Car Company in Sandusky, the *Sandusky Star-Journal* reported in 1915.

Dauch died in a car crash in August 1918 in the Sandusky area. Dauch's chauffeur also died, and Dauch's wife, daughter and another local businessman were hurt. Dauch was considered Sandusky's foremost manufacturer, according to his obituary in the *Star-Journal*. In addition to his businesses, he had contributed money to the Salvation Army and a local hospital and was president of the Sandusky Businessmen's Association, the *Register* reported.

"He was the wealthiest man in town, and the most important," historian Gordon Wendt told the *Register*.

Hinde died in February 1931 of pneumonia. His obituary in the *Register* referred to him as "father of the fibre package making industry of the United States."

Despite the deaths of its founders, Hinde and Dauch Paper Company continued to grow. In addition to shipping containers, it made colorful display stands for products and containers for products.

"For those unenlightened souls who believe that a paper box is just a paper box, a tour through the Hinde Dauch plant would be in the nature of a revelation," the *Star-Journal* reported in 1938. "Here, the whizzing machinery turns out hundreds of thousands of clever, distinctive display stands for such well known products as Palm Olive, Lux and Life Buoy Soaps, for Colgate products of all descriptions, shipping boxes for candles, baked confections, beer, whiskey, radios, rubber heels, lams [*sic*], butter and practically every item purchased as part of everyday living."

For decades, the company continued to make these types of products. Company brochures circa the 1950s show boxes for aftershave, paint, motor oil, canned corn and more. Stands included a Johnson & Johnson Band-Aid display. It also expanded into making insulation material for refrigerator cabinets for General Electric, Westinghouse and other companies, the *Star-Journal* reported in 1938.

In 1953, Hinde and Dauch Paper Company merged with the West Virginia Pulp and Paper Company, whose Westvaco Corporation ran the Sandusky plant. Charles Frohman, a well-known Sandusky historian, was the company's last president before the merger. In 1965, the company moved administrative groups to New York City and closed its office building at 407 Decatur Street.

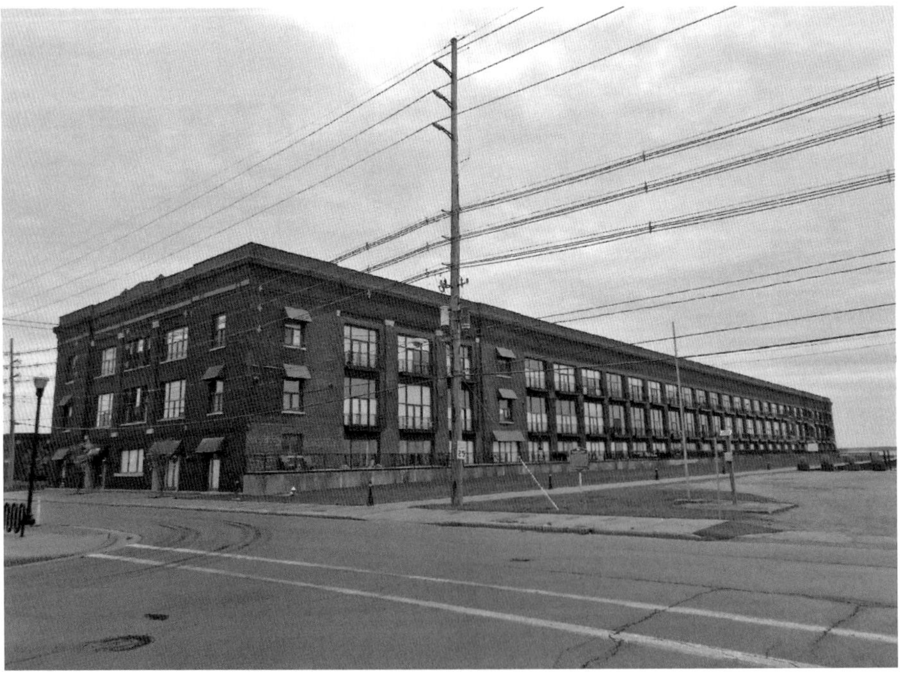

The Hinde and Dauch factory on Shoreline Drive (this was the last location of the factory before it closed) was converted into apartments. *Photo by Kristina Smith.*

The building was donated to the Sandusky City Schools Board of Education and still houses the school district's administrative offices.

"The overall profitability of the Sandusky operation has been less than satisfactory in the highly competitive environment in which we operate," H.E. Beeken, vice-president and manager of Westvaco's container division, told the *Register* in 1981.

Westvaco leased the plant to a competitor that year, and it changed hands one more time after that, going to its last owner, Chesapeake Corporation of Richmond, Virginia.

The plant closed in 1997. Two years later, the City of Sandusky bought the empty factory and, in 2003, partnered with a development company to turn the building into loft condos. The condos opened in 2007.

The factory building is listed on the National Register of Historic Places.

## Jackson Underwear Factory

Although underwear capital of the world was not one of Sandusky's many monikers, undergarments did play an important role in its manufacturing sector at the turn of the twentieth century.

The factory was unusual because it mostly employed women at a time when women hadn't yet broken into the workforce en masse. At that time, most of the jobs women could get were as servants, dress or hat makers or clerks, according to the *Register*.

A.H. Jackson—who would later serve as a U.S. congressman—had two thriving businesses in nearby Fremont: an underwear factory and the Jackson Knife and Cutlery Works. (Fremont was a hub for cutlery manufacturers at that time.) The underwear factory was doing so well that Jackson was falling behind on his orders and didn't have enough workers to fill them, according to the *Register*. Fremont was too small to offer any more workers, so he decided to start another factory in Sandusky at North Depot and McDonough Streets.

The Sandusky factory, however, did not make underwear. Instead, the workers made pajamas and nightgowns for women and children. Those garments were sold at Sears and Montgomery Ward stores.

"The women were paid by the piece, and the average wage was $5 per week," the newspaper reported. "Many Sandusky women learned to sew at the facility."

Labor disputes with a workers' union in the early '30s doomed the plant, which Jackson closed. Other businesses were located there briefly: Bontex, which made clothes; Store-Aid, which made wardrobes; and Flexible Conveyor, according to the newspaper. The building was torn down in 1963.

Today, there are houses on the site.

## Barr Rubber Products

From footballs and basketballs to dog toys and car parts, Barr Rubber Products made things people across the world use every day.

The company started in 1920 in Lorain, a city east of Sandusky, and was named after its first president, Nelt Barr. It first made balloons.

The company then moved to Sandusky in 1923 and opened at 424 East Market Street. After the move, Barr Rubber acquired Ravenna Rubber Products Company and added small, inflated balls to its product lines, according to the *Register*. It continued to expand its products and made large gas-inflated balls, dog toys and mechanical goods.

Business was going well when fire destroyed the plant in September 1928. But the fire did little to slow the company's output. It moved to the old Dauch Tractor Company, 1531 First Street, the following year and continued making balloons and toys, according to Sandusky Library Archives files.

Nine years later, Barr Rubber was making 5 million to 7 million balloons a year and 26 million balls a year, the *Star-Journal* reported in 1938. It also continued to make toys for dogs and found that giving them a vanilla flavor added to their popularity.

When the United States joined World War II, the company again added to its products. Barr Rubber made life rafts and fuel and oil tanks for the war effort, according to the *Register*. After the war, the company made balls and toys again.

Then in 1965, the company became part of Lancaster Colony Corporation of Columbus. It stopped making balloons and expanded its production of toy balls, athletic balls and family game sets, according to the *Register*. Company brochures show order forms where customers could choose from play balls with stars, stripes and other patterns in a rainbow of colors and basketballs, footballs and more that could be ordered to match the color of customers' team jerseys.

Barr Rubber's workforce peaked in 1973, when it had five hundred hourly workers, according to the *Register*. A strike that year, however, scared off customers, and the company soon laid off workers.

The company also changed its product line. Instead of making toys, it focused more on making car parts, like bumpers and conduits. By 1980, 80 percent of the company's business was focused on auto parts and vinyl boat bumpers, according to the *Register*. GM and Ford were among the larger customers. The remaining 20 percent of production was toys and balls.

Then business began to decline. Competition in the auto industry caused carmakers to cut expenses and production, which meant less work for Barr Rubber, according to the *Register*. Lancaster Colony Corporation decided to close the plant and consolidate its operation with other plants located elsewhere. The Sandusky plant had been losing money for two years, the newspaper reported. The last year Barr Rubber was listed in the city business directory was 1986.

Ted Lazar, Lancaster Colony Corporation vice-president, told the *Register* that cuts in the auto industry contributed to the decision to close.

"But the chief reason for the losses at Barr, he said, is because the plant is not modernized and cannot manufacture its products cheaper and faster than the competition," the newspaper reported. "The problem runs a vicious circle: Obsolete production methods and equipment have led to the losses, which leaves no money for modernization."

Today, the factory is gone, and the lot is empty.

## Sandusky Portland Cement Company

In the 1860s and '70s, Columbia University chemistry professor John Strong Newberry did a geological survey of Ohio. In the area of Bay View, a village west of Sandusky, he found a type of stone, called marl, which was used in making cement.

In 1892, his three sons—Arthur, Spencer and William Newberry—decided to take advantage of the large deposits of marl in the area, the *Lorain Morning Journal* reported. They opened the Sandusky Portland Cement Company along the Sandusky Bay in a small burg known then as Bay Bridge, which was near Bay View.

Marl was a critical element of a certain type of cement, called Portland cement, which likely led to the Portland part of the company's name. The area also had plenty of clay, another main ingredient in cement.

In 1927, the company name changed to Medusa Portland Cement Company, named after the character in Greek mythology, according to the

*Register*. Medusa had beautiful hair, and she compared her locks to those of goddess Minerva. That statement enraged Minerva, who used her powers to turn Medusa's lustrous locks into hissing snakes. Medusa became so hideous that anyone who looked at her turned to stone.

Thus, Medusa seemed like a good name to affiliate with a cement company. The business's logo featured Medusa's face, complete with her snake hair.

The company thrived and made cement that was the foundation of many roads and buildings. During the post–World War II building boom of the 1950s, the company posted record years, the *Journal* reported. The factory employed many local residents of Bay Bridge and Bay View, including immigrants, according to the *Register*. It was considered the oldest cement plant in Ohio, according to the newspaper.

But like anything mined, the supply of marl was finite. The local deposits were diminished to the point that the plant could no longer make cement, according to the *Register*. It closed in 1960. The facility served as a cement storage building for a while.

## Jarecki Chemical Company

In the late 1800s and early 1900s, Sandusky had the largest fish market in the world. Sturgeon, whitefish, perch and pickerel (today called walleye on the U.S. side of the lake) were so prevalent that several fish companies caught and shipped them to eager markets.

With this bumper crop of fish came plenty of waste. Not all of the fish were edible, and there were five thousand to six thousand tons a year of parts left over after the fish were filleted, the *Register* reported in 1896.

Seeing these fish guts as an opportunity, the Jarecki Chemical Company formed in 1878. Located at 1509 First Street, it ground the refuse into fertilizer, called fish guano. It was the only manufacturer of this substance west of the Atlantic coast, according to the newspaper.

The company used raw bone, fish scraps, sulfuric acid and more as nutrients that would help plants grow. Fish that people wouldn't eat—sheepshead and dogfish that got stuck in the commercial anglers' nets—were turned into fertilizer. A trained chemist was on-site to make sure the fertilizer was made correctly.

Fish guano was one of few types of manure that could be safely applied to plants at seeding time, the *Register* reported.

"Farm-yard manure is so slowly available in the soil that it must be applied in considerable excess; but fish manure seems to just keep up with the needs of the growing plant," according to the newspaper.

Armour Agricultural Chemical Company, a division of Armour Foods, later bought the company. Armour closed the plant in July 1964 for undisclosed reasons, the *Register* reported that year.

Although Sandusky Bay and Lake Erie remain excellent fisheries, Sandusky has not had the largest fish market in the world for decades. Overfishing decimated the populations of sturgeon—endangered in Ohio—whitefish and other species.

The U.S. Fishery Commission and Ohio Department of Natural Resources set limits on how many of certain types of fish can be harvested each year from the Ohio waters of Lake Erie, and the federal agency's reach extends into other Lake Erie states' waters. Biologists across the lake monitor fish populations to give input on the quotas. When Jarecki Chemical opened, there were no limits on how many fish could be taken from the lake.

Today, the factory is gone, and the lot is empty.

## Sandusky Tool Company

In the early days of woodworking, tools called plane irons were used to make different pieces of woodwork that fitted together. Making different pieces required different plane irons. The devices were used to make grooves for tongue and groove work, according to *Americana* magazine.

For decades, the Sandusky Tool Company helped meet demand for these irons, and by 1905, it made two-thirds of the plane irons used in America and sent shipments to other countries, the *Register* reported.

The company was located at 146 Meigs Street, where Battery Park is today. The city initially had dedicated the land where the factory was located, called East Battery, as a site for American cannons to defend Sandusky against a potential British attack, wrote Wilbert Schwer, Sandusky Tool Company secretary, in a history of the company he compiled in 1967. But relations with Britain had improved, and the site was never fortified, Schwer wrote.

The city set aside the property for a shipyard, but that never developed either. A sawmill was located on the site for a while, and then a woodworking plant opened there in 1868, Schwer wrote. A company called Allen, Dorsey and Tenney made wood planes for tool handles.

The following year, the Sandusky Tool Company was incorporated and took over Allen, Dorsey and Tenney. The city leased the land to the Sandusky Tool Company, and the company began expanding sales. It brought J.A. Montgomery from the Ohio Tool Company in Columbus to be the plant's superintendent, according to Montgomery's obituary in the *Register* in 1899.

"Mr. Montgomery must have been one of the true mechanical geniuses of his day, and at least in his field, for he designed some ingenious woodworking machinery that was thereafter used throughout the life of the tool company for performing some of the intricate operations involved in manufacturing wood planes," Schwer wrote in the company history.

In addition to plane irons, the company made hoes. It ran into some trouble with the type of hoe used in the 1800s, called an eye hoe, according to Schwer's history. That hoe involved a few pieces that did not hold together after heavy use. Electrical arc welding didn't exist at that time, so the pieces could not be welded together, leaving the company unsure of what to do.

Enter Schwer's grandfather, Albert Schwer. His family ran a blacksmith shop in Sandusky, and he could make an eye hoe forged from a single piece of steel, which eliminated the problem of the pieces coming apart. He went to work for the company and made the machines the company used to manufacture the eye hoe he designed, according to Wilbert Schwer's history.

Wood construction was prevalent during that era, so the company had plenty of business, Wilbert Schwer wrote. The company also made wood screws and mallets, specialty tools for the cooperage trade, saw handles and more, according to an 1896 advertisement published in the *Register*.

"The best of mechanical resources enable us to turn out the most perfect and artistic tools in the world, and we manufacture to order all kinds of specialties in the shape of tools," according to the ad.

By the time World War I broke out, however, the company was becoming increasingly unprofitable, Wilbert Schwer wrote in his history. Newer technology was making the tool company's products out of date. In June 1924, a tornado ripped through Sandusky and damaged all the company's buildings, temporarily shuttering the business.

Wilbert Schwer's father, George Schwer, and William Seitz then took over the company. George Schwer was president, and Seitz was vice-president. Wilbert Schwer was named secretary. They repaired the company's buildings and started operations again in 1925, according to Wilbert Schwer's history. Still, Sandusky Tool Company was one of two companies left in the country that made wood planes. The company could not escape that the product was becoming obsolete, Wilbert Schwer wrote. So it changed its product lines and kept making hoes.

"We sent out vast quantities of our attractive new catalogues with high hopes, but our hopes were not sufficiently realized," Wilbert Schwer wrote. "We soon came face to face with the grim fact that we were manufacturing a fine line of carriages, buggy whips, fly nets, harness and sleigh bells in an automotive age."

The company's lease with the city also was running out, and negotiations to extend it failed. The owners sold the company in 1926 to American Fork and Hoe Company, which renamed the plant the Sandusky Tool Corporation. Over the years, equipment was taken away from the plant, and it stopped making hoes. The company closed in 1931.

The buildings and lease were sold to the city, and the buildings were torn down. A baseball field was built on the site.

# 4
# HOTELS

## Hotel Rieger

In 1912, one of Sandusky's most luxurious hotels opened at the corner of Jackson and Market Streets. Hotel Rieger had sixty rooms, was considered fireproof and had all the modern conveniences a guest could want, including running water. Some rooms even had adjoining bathrooms, according to the *Sandusky Star-Journal*.

Ornate woodwork decorated the lobby, and guests could take an elevator or the elegant marble and iron staircase up to their rooms. The four-story brick building had a basement and space for shops on the first floor.

"Hundreds and hundreds of people who passed through the new Hotel Rieger Wednesday afternoon, admiring its completeness and its beauty at every turn, agreed that nowhere in the state can be found a more beautiful hotel of its size, or even considerably larger," the *Star-Journal* reported on May 1, 1912. "From the entrance to the beautiful lobby, up and back to the last room on the fourth floor, it is as near perfection as could be devised—a credit alike to its designer, builders, owners and the city. That it was designed, built and furnished by Sandusky people, is something of which Sanduskians can be proud."

The man who built and owned the hotel was Edward F. Rieger, who was already considered successful in the hotel business for his work at other establishments, the newspaper reported. The hotel did well and expanded in 1915 and 1916.

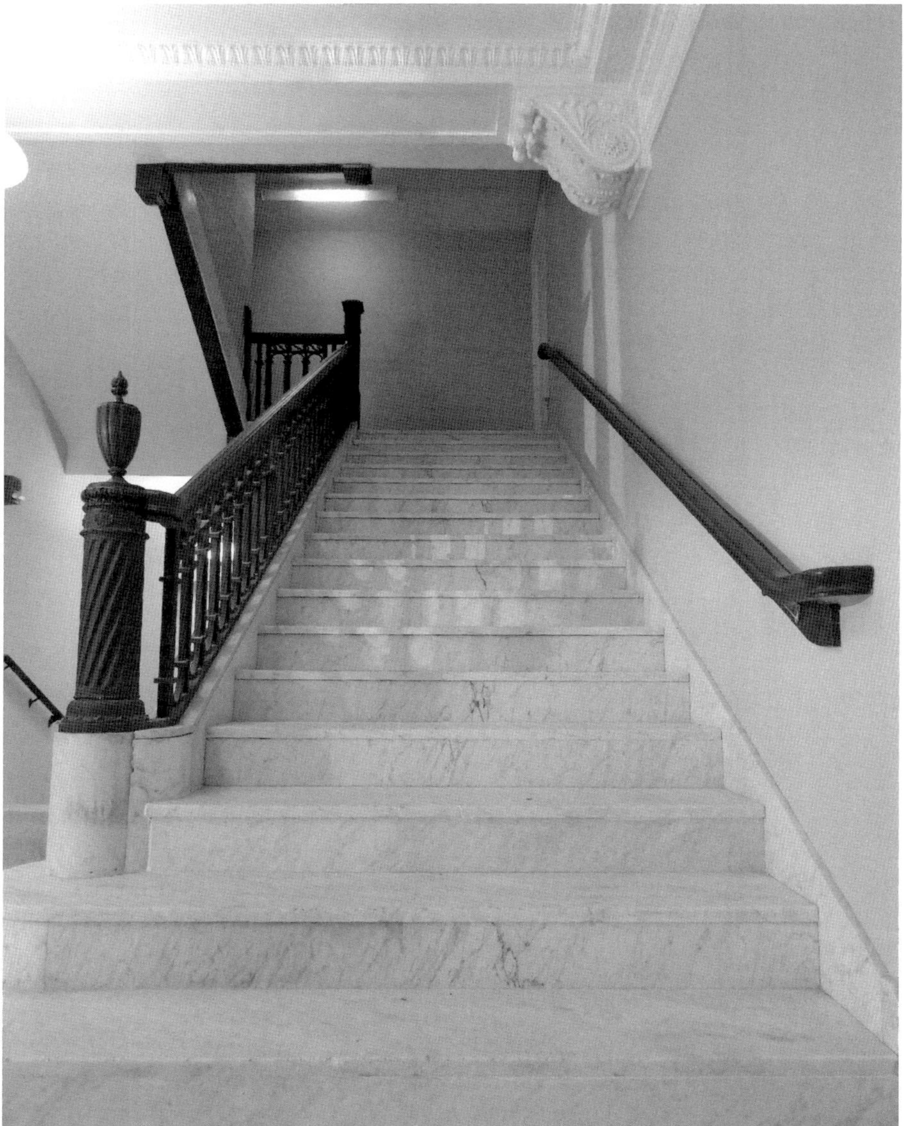

The marble stairs from the Rieger's glory days as a hotel are still there. *Photo by Kristina Smith.*

Rieger ran the hotel until he died in 1921 after falling from a fourth-floor window there, according to the *Star-Journal*. He was thirty-nine.

After his death, his family added on to the building and renovated it. In 1926, they opened the new Hotel Rieger and promoted it as the finest hotel in Ohio, the newspaper reported. The building included three dining rooms, a coffee shop, a lounge and ice-making machines. The top floors offered views of the city and Lake Erie.

"Every one of the 150 rooms has been newly decorated and furnished as have the halls, the appearance of the entire interior is that of a new building then, too, the fine system of forced air ventilation, installed at a great expense, causes an atmosphere of freshness, which is apparent upon entering the building," the *Star-Journal* reported on June 9, 1926. "This is particularly noticeable in the kitchen by the absence of the odors from cooking."

Stores on the first floor over the years included Bamberger's Hat Shop, a barbershop and a beauty shop, the *Register* reported. A travel agency, a tailor and a notary also set up shop there, according to the newspaper.

The hotel changed hands in 1964 and was renamed the Erie Inn Motor Hotel. It had a popular dining hall, where service clubs had meetings and downtown workers stopped for lunch, the *Register* reported.

Five years later, the hotel's fifth floor was converted into a nursing home. In 1982, the entire hotel became a nursing home, which stayed open for five years.

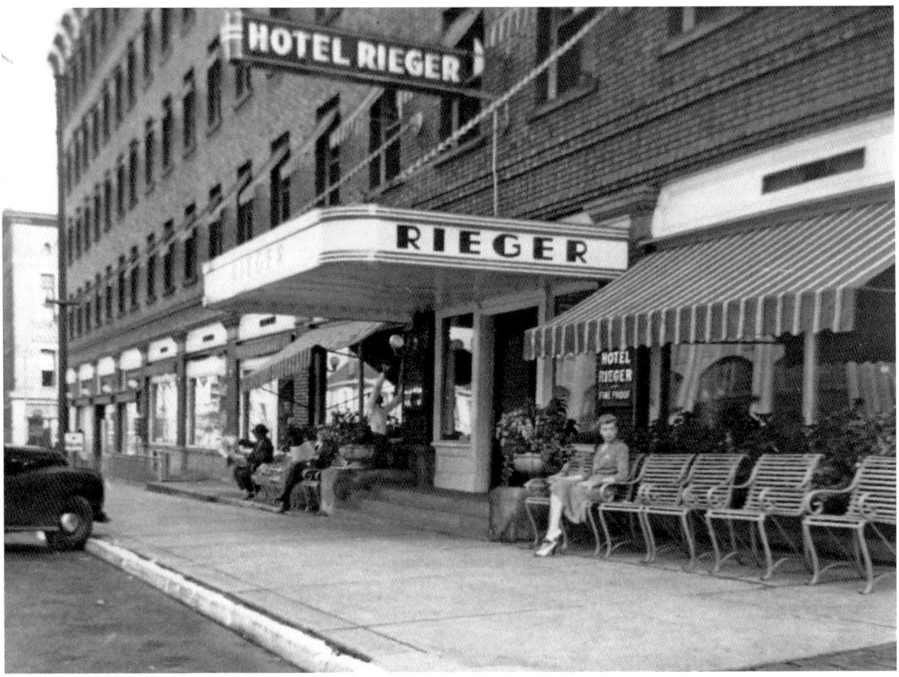


The Hotel Rieger as it appeared in 1942. *Sandusky Library Follett House Museum Archives.*

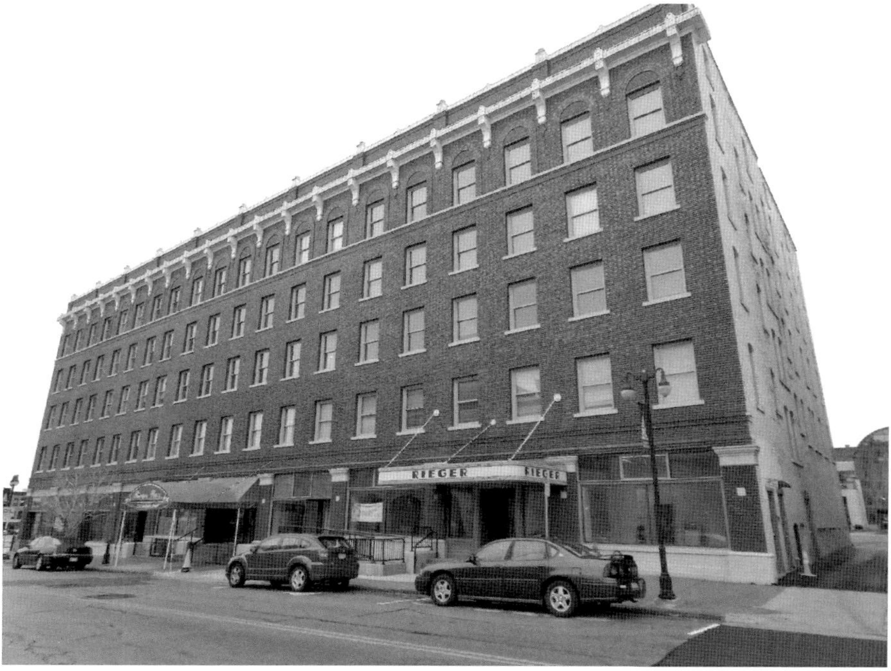


The Hotel Rieger is now an apartment complex. *Photo by Kristina Smith.*

The next venture at the historic building would be a short-lived bed-and-breakfast. Fourteen of the rooms were opened as a clean, quiet "Christian atmosphere for vacationing families," the *Register* reported. The basement still had businesses then, including a beauty shop and a tattoo parlor.

By 1996, financial problems had caused the bed-and-breakfast and shops to leave, and the building sat empty. The building fell into disrepair, and it was the subject of a paranormal investigation before its latest owner decided to renovate it and turn it into apartments for senior citizens, according to the *Register*.

Rieger Place Apartments opened in 2014. The original woodwork and marble staircase are still there, and original room doors still line the upstairs hallways.

Renovation continued during the fall of 2014 as the first residents moved in, and a library, craft room and banquet hall were planned for the building. The owners planned to lease the first-floor area for shops and businesses, said Dina Heyman, who works for the company managing the apartments.

"They're very popular," she said of the apartments. "A lot of people are selling their houses and moving here."

Residents include a man who was a bellhop at the Hotel Rieger and another man who stayed at the hotel on his honeymoon, she said. The building is on the National Register of Historic Places.

## Exchange Hotel: Charles Dickens Stayed Here

Of Sandusky's historic hotels, the Exchange might be the most famous because of its best-known visitor: British author Charles Dickens.

The Exchange was at the corner of Wayne and Water Streets, and it had a number of names over the years, including Colt's Exchange, St. Lawrence Hotel, the Geiersdorf, Wayne and Porterhouse. The brick structure was built in 1837 and was first known as the Exchange. Guests at the time included settlers who stopped in Sandusky on their way to the West, according to the *Lorain Morning Journal.*

Dickens spent one night of his 1842 tour of the United States at the hotel, which was then known as Colt's Exchange. His visit sparked stories that persist today—not all of them true. Mary Wilcoxon, who was a child at the time, recalled the visit in an interview with the *Star-Journal* in 1922.

Instead of meeting with the crowd that waited for him at the train stop on Wayne Street, Dickens waited until after dark to leave the train and enter the hotel, Wilcoxon told the newspaper. By then, the crowd was gone.

Wilcoxon was in the crowd and was disappointed she didn't get to see Dickens. She thought she'd get another chance at a dinner in Dickens's honor, but he declined to attend because he didn't want to hear a bunch of long speeches, she told the *Star-Journal.*

"So I began to cry, and cried so hard that father took me from the banquet room up to the parlor where he sat down upon a sofa trying to comfort my girlish heart, for my father was a very kind man," she told the newspaper. "I was sitting on my father's lap when the parlor door opened and a pleasant faced lady came out and asked my father what I was crying about.

"My father did not know who she was and told her my desire to see Mr. Dickens and how I felt my childish disappointment."

Neither Wilcoxon nor her father knew it, but the woman was Dickens's wife. She then led Wilcoxon into the room, where Dickens greeted her and talked with her about his stories, which she had read.

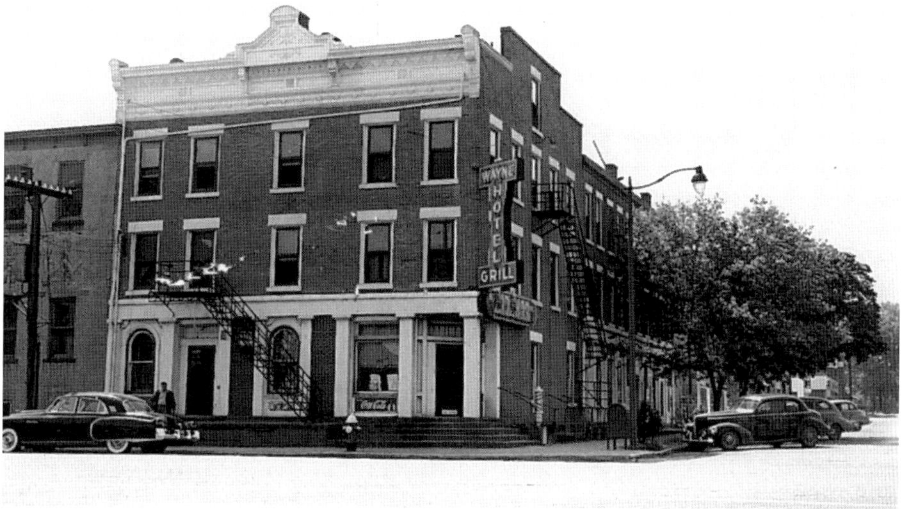


Charles Dickens stayed at the Exchange Hotel, later called the Wayne Hotel. It is pictured in this 1951 photo by Clarence Fuller. *Sandusky Library Follett House Museum Archives.*

"I spent perhaps half an hour in his room, which has always remained one of the pleasantest memories of my life," Wilcoxon told the *Star-Journal.* "He gave me an English sixpence to remember him by."

Dickens also told her she was the only person he had spoken with in Sandusky. His writings in his *American Notes* indicate that he wasn't overly fond of the town but found his host at the hotel, proprietor R.E. Colt, to be attentive and hospitable.

"We put up at a comfortable little hotel on the brink of Lake Erie; lay there that night and had no choice but to wait there the next day until a steam boat bound for Buffalo appeared," Dickens wrote. "The town, which was sluggish and un-interesting enough, was something like the back of an English watering-place out of season."

Dickens's story sparked another piece of Sandusky lore that has long since been found to be false. Legend has it that when Dickens stopped in Buffalo, he asked for a steak like the one "Porter served him in Sandusky," thus giving the Porterhouse steak its name, the *Star-Journal* reported in 1923.

The story doesn't add up. There was a Porterhouse Hotel in Sandusky around that time period, but it was across the street from Colt's Exchange. And the Porterhouse's proprietor, a man by the name of Porter, didn't

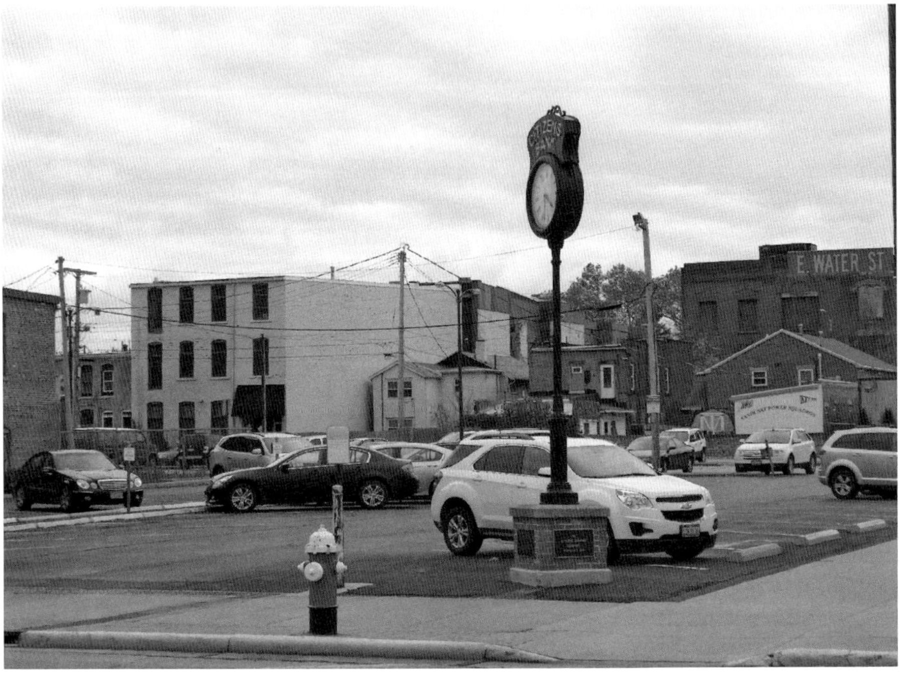


A bank parking lot is located where the Exchange Hotel once stood. *Photo by Kristina Smith.*

take over that hotel until at least a year after Dickens's visit, the newspaper reported. Colt's Exchange wouldn't be called the Porterhouse until after 1958. Nor does Dickens say anything in *American Notes* about eating a steak in Sandusky.

"And so regretfully, Sandusky must relinquish the hope of giving to the world so noble a masterpiece as the 'Porterhouse steak,'" the newspaper said.

A few years later, the hotel—known as the St. Lawrence at that time—was used as a hospital during a cholera epidemic in the city, the *Register* reported. Then during the Civil War, the hotel was a barracks for Union troops. Later, the building housed a candy factory and then a nightclub.

In 1977, a fire gutted the hotel—last known as the Porterhouse—and the building was condemned. Locals tried for years to restore and save the hotel, which was listed on the National Register of Historic Places, according to records on file in the Sandusky Library Archives. Renovation never happened, and the building was torn down in 1985. Today, the spot where the hotel stood is a parking lot for Citizens Bank.

## Steamboat Hotel

The Steamboat Hotel was located across Wayne Street from the Exchange, and it was sometimes confused with the Exchange as the place where Dickens stayed. That could be because each hotel was called the Porterhouse at one time.

Cyrus Marsh built the Steamboat in 1817, but he first called it Marsh's Tavern, according to Hewson L. Peeke's *A Standard History of Erie County Vol. 1*. It was the first hotel in Sandusky and the second frame building erected there, according to Sandusky Library Archives. In 1818, the hotel was renamed the Steamboat because Lake Erie's first steamboat, *Walk-in-the-Water*, started running that year, according to *A Standard History*. The Steamboat Hotel was the favored place to stay in the early 1830s, Peeke wrote in this book.

In the 1840s, proprietor Alexander T. Porter put a verandah around the front of the building and changed its name to the Verandah Hotel. Over the years, the hotel was named the Porterhouse (presumably after Porter), Raymond's Hotel, Scott's American and the New Lake House, according to newspaper accounts.

In 1885, it was the New Lake House, and it had twenty-one "sleeping apartments" considered comfortable and well furnished, the *Register* reported. The hotel was conveniently close to railroad depots and steamship docks.

"The house fronts on the Bay giving from the north rooms a good view of our harbor and its surroundings," the newspaper reported.

When the hotel was torn down in 1923, it was reputed to be the oldest building in Sandusky. Today, Citizens Bank stands on the lot that once housed the Steamboat Hotel.

## West House

The West House, a five-story stone building at the corner of Water Street and Columbus Avenue, opened in 1858. The opening was just in time to house visitors to the state fair, which was being held in Sandusky that year. At one time, it was considered the largest hotel between Cleveland and Toledo, the *Register* reported.

In 1885, the hotel was a favorite among visitors and had been recently improved, the *Register* reported.

"Many of the rooms present a magnificent view of the bay, and the great lake to be seen in the distance, an ever varying scene upon which the eye never tires," the newspaper said.

The West House abruptly closed in September 1914. The widow of owner Joseph Wagner closed it for financial reasons, the *Register* reported. The last person to stay there was a railroad conductor, according to the newspaper.

The hotel was torn down in 1919. The State Theatre stands in its place.

## Sloane House

Sloane House stood out from others because of its ornate Victorian architecture. Rush R. Sloane built the five-story brick structure in 1880 at the corner of Washington Row and Columbus Avenue. Sloane was a prominent businessman, lawyer, president of a local railroad and advocate for the Underground Railroad that had several stops in Sandusky. He also served as a judge and the city's mayor.

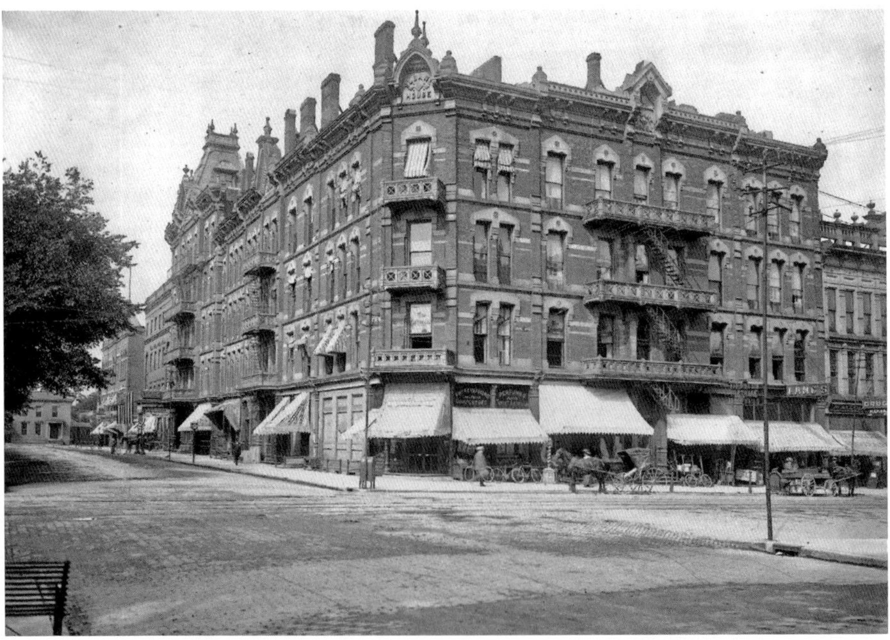

The Sloane House Hotel was a good example of Victorian architecture. The LaSalle department store took its place. *Sandusky Library Follett House Museum Archives.*

The brick building was one of the best examples in the city of Victorian architecture. Inside, it had narrow hallways and wide staircases.

When it opened, the hotel was so successful that it expanded farther down the block, and the area around it was called Sloane Block, according to the *Register*. Jewelry stores and specialty shops filled the building's first floor.

"The Sloane House is the finest block in our city, built of stone, iron and brick, the architectural beauty being of the highest order and the arrangements within and without of the most complete design," the *Register* reported in 1885.

At that time, the hotel had 120 rooms and boasted "luxuriously furnished reception rooms" and "superb parlors," according to the newspaper.

When Hotel Rieger was built in 1912, it hurt Sloane House's business, according to the *Register*. In its later years, Sloane House was a boardinghouse and was frequented by visitors to Cedar Point, historian Virginia Steinemann told the newspaper.

"I suppose it was elegant in its way," Steinemann told the *Register* of the hotel's later years. "It was an enormous building. It looked neat from the outside."

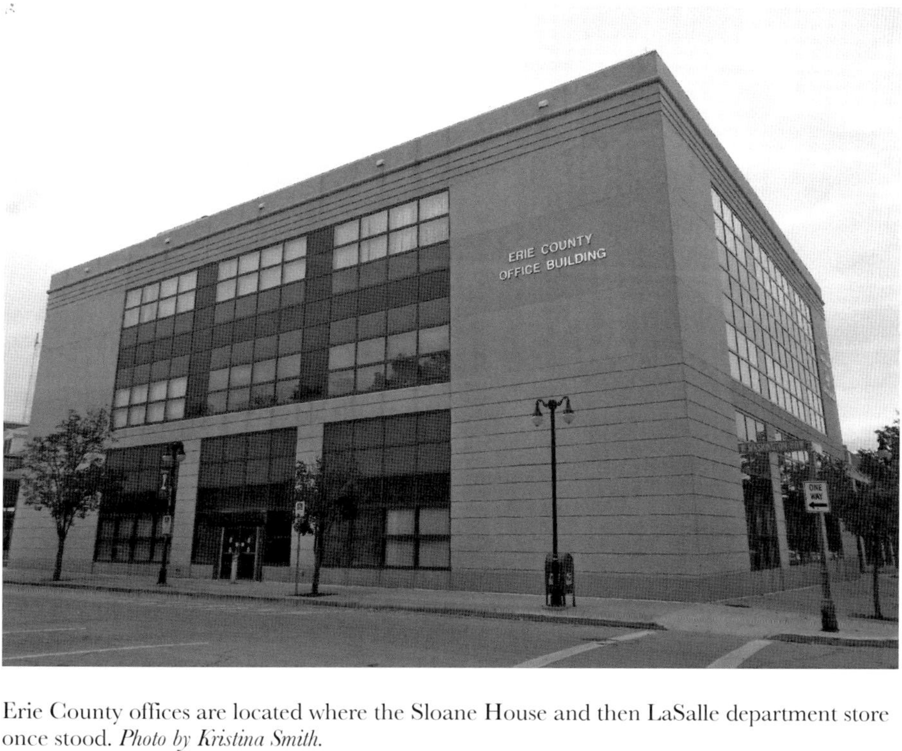


Erie County offices are located where the Sloane House and then LaSalle department store once stood. *Photo by Kristina Smith.*

Sloane House was torn down in two phases, said Ron Davidson, Sandusky Library special collections librarian. The first phase was in 1948, and the demolition made way for the LaSalle department store, which was a division of the J.H. Macy Co.

The rest of the building fell into disrepair, and the city ordered it to be torn down after two upper stories collapsed in 1957 and buried part of a neighboring jewelry store in debris, according to Sandusky Library Archives files. Washington Row was closed to traffic because of concerns about the building's instability. The rest of the building was torn down that year, according to the *Register*.

LaSalle closed in 1982, and Erie County offices are now located on the site.

"This was just a way of life that is gone forever," Steinemann told the *Register* of Sloane House. "You will never see a building like that again."

# 5
# CEDAR POINT

## The Lost Island, College Research Lab and More

Long before it became the largest amusement park in the world, Cedar Point was a wild stretch of land along the Sandusky Bay. Covered with trees—including cedars, which is how it got its name—it was home to wild animals that roamed the seven-mile-long peninsula. American Indians and white settlers hunted and fished there.

In 1821, it was still an untamed forest with a long, sandy beach, according to Hewson L. Peeke's *The Centennial History of Erie County, Ohio, Vol. 1*.

Joseph Gaspard Chaussegros de Léry, the French explorer who reported finding the Port Clinton Fort Sandusky, also made note in his journals of seeing "Point aux Cedres" in 1754, according to the *Historical Society of Northwestern Ohio Quarterly Bulletin* published in 1937.

Through the years, Cedar Point would be a setting for some diverse historical events.

It was the safe haven for a group of United States soldiers who American Indians ambushed on the nearby Marblehead Peninsula during the first Ohio battle of the War of 1812. Outnumbered, some soldiers escaped to Cedar Point and came back to rescue the survivors in the fight, known as the Skirmish on the Peninsula, the *Port Clinton News Herald* reported in 2013.

About one hundred years later, in 1913, Notre Dame quarterback Knute Rockne and fellow lifeguard and friend Charles "Gus" Dorias perfected the forward pass there, which set football on its way to becoming the game we watch today.

The first American long-distance flight over water ended at Cedar Point on August 10, 1931. Glenn Curtiss flew sixty-four miles from Cleveland over Lake Erie to Cedar Point, eclipsing a twenty-five-mile flight a French aviator made over the English Channel, according to the *Sandusky Register*.

Decades later, Cedar Point would become known as America's Roller Coast and house some of the biggest and fastest coasters in the world.

Before all of this happened, enterprising people saw the land's picturesque location and access to the lake as a potential moneymaker. They started Cedar Point on its way to becoming a tourist destination.

During the 1840s, commercial fishermen set up shop there. Then in 1849, landowner N.M. Porter advertised that anyone who wanted to fish on Cedar Point must give him one-eighth of the catch, according to *The Centennial History of Erie County, Ohio, Vol. 1*.

Eight years later, the *Sandusky Register* wrote an editorial suggesting that someone open a bathhouse on Cedar Point:

> *There is no finer place in the world than the spot mentioned. The beach is broad, and of the finest and whitest sand; the bottom of the lake is smooth as a house floor, and slopes gradually to any desired depth of water; the lake water is of the purest blue, and the "swells" simply glorious. A bathing-house, which would answer every purpose, could be built at trifling cost, and would be sure to pay a good dividend on the investment. Will not some enterprising person give us a bathing-house?*

Louis Zistel obliged in 1870 and built a beer garden with a dance floor and a bathhouse. Other bathhouses and a dance hall followed, and in 1887, the Cedar Point Pleasure Resort Company was formed.

"Sanduskians began to enjoy their resort by forming parties and excursions to Cedar Point," Peeke wrote in *The Centennial History of Erie County, Ohio, Vol. 1*. "The steamboat *Hayes* made frequent trips, and the bay was aflutter with white-winged sailing vessels through the summer months.

"So popular did Cedar Point become that boats could scarcely be supplied to meet the demand, and new and better sailing craft were added to the stock on hand."

From there, a boardwalk, hotels, rides and other buildings of amusement were erected, sometimes displacing earlier constructions.

## Lighthouse

As commerce and travel on the Sandusky Bay grew, locals realized a lighthouse was needed to help guide the ships. Prominent Sandusky resident Eleutheros Cooke wrote a paper in 1832 to demonstrate the need for lights in the bay and at the mouths of the Huron and Black Rivers east of Sandusky, the *Sandusky Star-Journal* reported in 1902. A steamer left Sandusky for Buffalo, New York, each morning, and another departed for Detroit each afternoon, Cooke wrote. And the number of steamers was expected to increase.

"Many of the nights are dark and stormy, and great delay, distress, and frequent losses are occasioned for want of lights at these harbors," Cooke wrote. "The expense of their erection bears no comparison to the benefit they confer."

In 1837, an act of Congress appropriated $2,500 to build a lighthouse near the entrance of the Sandusky Bay at Cedar Point, historian Gordon Wendt wrote in the *Register* in 1990. A year later, that amount increased to $3,000 to finish the building. The lighthouse went into service in 1839.

This lighthouse marked the eastern edge of the Sandusky Bay. The Marblehead Lighthouse on the Marblehead Peninsula marked the western edge of the bay.

Through the years, at least two other beacons, called range lights, were built to further assist ships in navigating the area, according to various newspaper articles and *Lighthouse Digest* magazine. One of them was built in 1895, according to the *Star-Journal*. There is some confusion about when each light was built and where each was located, and newspaper articles of the day do not differentiate between the range lights.

Frank Ritter was the keeper of some of these lights. He tended them from 1892 to 1929, the *Star-Journal* reported in 1929, the year he retired.

Each year, his family lived in one of the range lights from March through much of December, presumably because the lake froze for the winter around that time. The house and beacon were built on a crib about a quarter mile off shore at Cedar Point. The house had a small yard and was otherwise surrounded by ten to twenty-five feet of water, according to Ritter's obituary in the *Register* in 1953. The family later moved out of the range light and into a house on the Cedar Point shore, according to the *Register*.

Ritter's wife often sat up watching for ships with him, according to multiple newspaper accounts. In those days, oil was used to light lamps, and the Ritters needed to trim the wicks and keep the lamps filled.

One night, the Ritters saw distress flares from a boat on the bay. There was no way to call the Marblehead Lighthouse and adjoining lifesaving station—the precursor to the U.S. Coast Guard—on the other side of the bay, so Frank Ritter rowed there in a lifeboat. He and other rescuers saved thirty to forty men and one woman that night, and everyone aboard the boat in trouble survived, according to Ritter's obituary.

Some of the lights were discontinued in 1904, according to *Lighthouse Digest*. The government kept one of the range light buildings for storing supplies, such as stakes and buoys, the *Register* reported in April 1904. Then in July 1910, that range light building caught fire and was destroyed, the *Star-Journal* reported. Some believed fireworks shot off by the steamer *Eastland*, which was leaving the dock at the time, started the blaze, according to the *Register*.

The U.S. Coast Guard had a station at one of the lighthouses until 1976, according to the *Register*. In 1987, Cedar Point bought the lighthouse and surrounding land and buildings for $425,000, the newspaper reported. It is not clear whether this was the original lighthouse or a range light. Cedar Point's website says that particular lighthouse was built in 1882, which would indicate it was not the original structure.

Cedar Point restored the lighthouse and built a family-style resort, called Lighthouse Point, around it.

## Hotels

Cedar Point's first hotel was the Bay Shore hotel, briefly known as the Hotel Villa. It was built in the late 1800s. The hotel had twenty rooms that quickly were completely booked, making the hotel an immediate success that was already too small to meet demand.

Next, the White House was built in 1901. This fifty-five-room lodging faced the lake, included porches and cost $100,000 to build, according to the book *Cedar Point: Queen of American Water Places* by David W. Francis and Diane DeMali Francis.

In 1915, the White House was added to the new hotel, the Cedars. It had a reputation as a quiet, secluded place to stay, according to *A Summertime Tradition on Lake Erie*, a DVD released by Cedar Point outlining highlights of the park's history. The Tiffany stained-glass windows that once decorated the Cedars are now part of the Breakers Hotel, the more than one-hundred-year-old grand building that remains Cedar Point's flagship hotel.

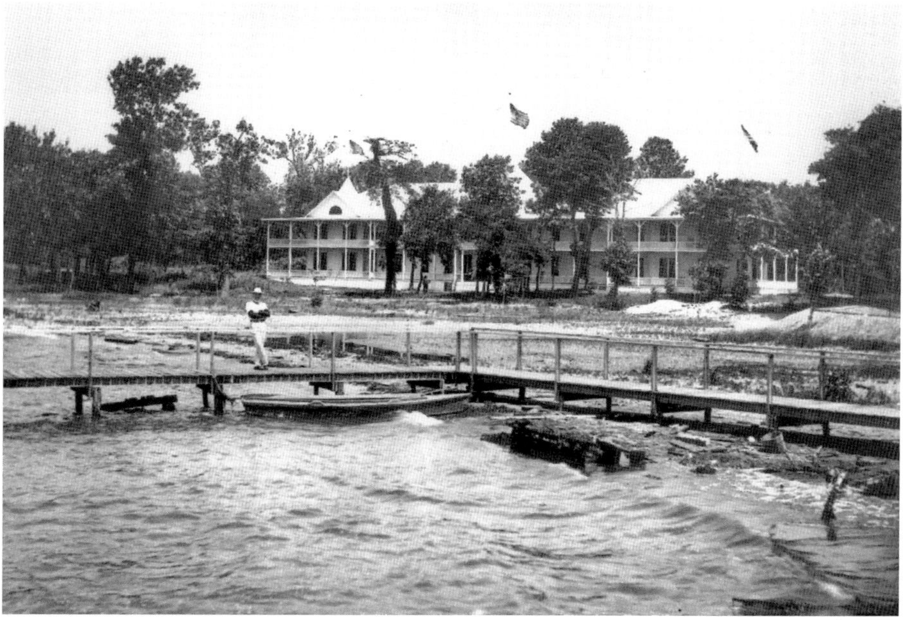

The White House was one of Cedar Point's first hotels. *Rutherford B. Hayes Presidential Center/ Charles Frohman Collection.*

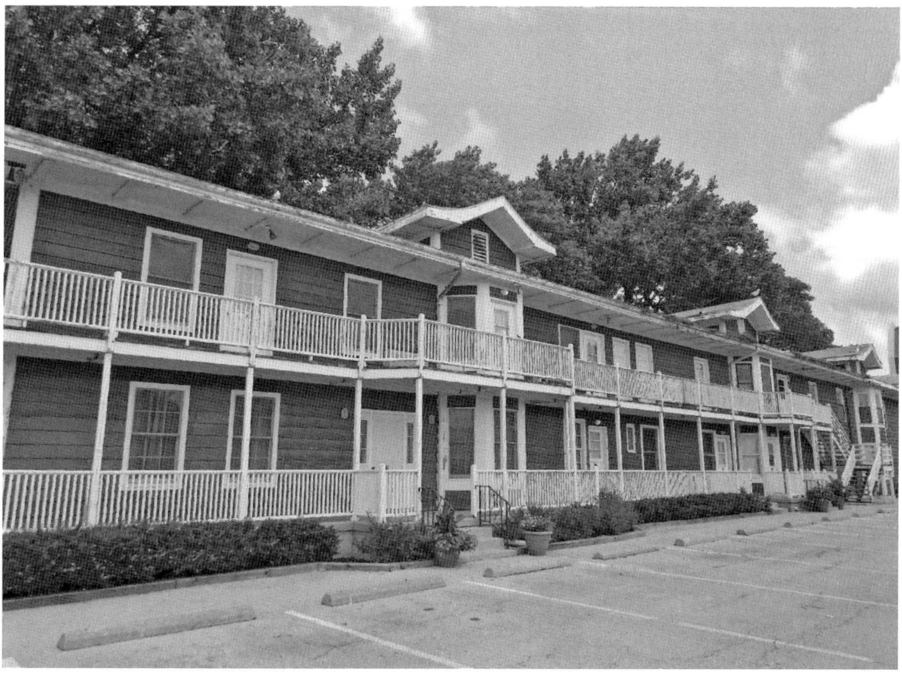

The White House and Cedars were converted into employee dorms. *Photo by Kristina Smith.*

Today, the White House and Cedars still stand by the Cedar Point Marina. The building is painted red and is used as a dormitory for summer employees.

## Ohio State University Lake Laboratory

On a small rock island a few hundred feet from popular South Bass Island tourist town Put-in-Bay sits Ohio State University's Franz Theodore Stone Laboratory.

Stone Lab on Gibraltar Island is the oldest freshwater biological research station in the United States, and it's a place where scientists and students from Ohio State and other universities study Lake Erie and its biology. Students take classes there, and researchers tackle a wide range of topics involving Lake Erie and its ecosystem.

Before the lab was on "The Rock," it was located in Sandusky and known as Lake Laboratory. It opened in 1895 at a fish hatchery in Sandusky. When

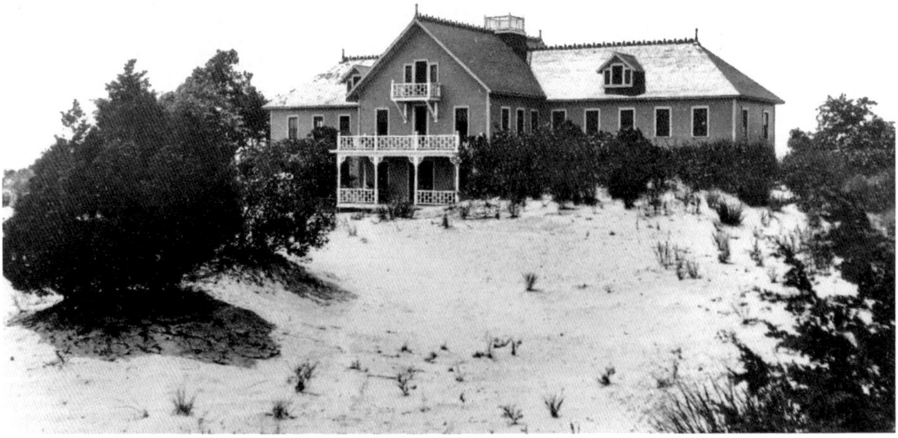

Ohio State University moved its Lake Laboratory to Cedar Point in 1903. The building was torn down after the lab was moved to Put-in-Bay. *Photo courtesy of Ohio State University's Ohio Sea Grant.*

it outgrew that space, OSU constructed a new building in 1903 at the end of Biemiller's Cove at Cedar Point at a cost of $3,376, according to Stone Lab's website. The building was constructed about half a mile south of the resort grounds, and it was officially opened during a ceremony on July 2, 1903, the *Register* reported the following day.

Back then, the lab's mission was similar to what it is today. The lab "is designed to provide a meeting ground for teachers and students of biology, to afford opportunity for the investigation of biology of the lake region, and for giving certain courses of instruction in biological subjects," according to a 1912 bulletin OSU published to promote the lab. Today, the lab also has special programs to educate groups, from charter boat captains to legislators to schoolchildren on field trips, about Lake Erie, its ecosystem and challenges to the lake's health.

Cedar Point was an ideal location for the lab because it was near a variety of areas that would be study subjects: marshes, a forest, rivers, a sandy beach and rocky islands. The lab building could accommodate at least one hundred people and was equipped with microscopes, a dark room, "carefully selected" books and other equipment, according to the 1912 bulletin.

Students could choose from several courses, including zoology, ichthyology (study of fish), entomology (study of insects), ornithology (study of birds) and aquatic biology. They studied fishes of Ohio, dragonflies, birds and water snakes, the *Sandusky Star-Journal* reported in July 1909. The lab became known as the "Bug House," according to the *Star-Journal*.

"The sight of students, and spectacled professors of stern countenance chasing bugs with long handled nets gave the summer school its local name," the newspaper reported.

Students came from across the country and as far as Calcutta, India, to study there, the *Star-Journal* reported.

The growing amusement park, however, began to encroach on quiet areas the students needed for study, and it would eventually need the space as its attractions grew, said Ken Miller, a fourteen-year Cedar Point employee who works in the park's Town Hall Museum.

The resort was dumping sewage into Biemiller's Cove, an area on the peninsula that students studied, according to *Queen of American Watering Places*. Sewage did nothing to help the ecosystem.

And summer cottages sprang up, bringing people and cars that also took habitat from the creatures the students at Lake Lab studied, the *Star-Journal* reported in 1920. Additionally, Cedar Point's manager at the time, George

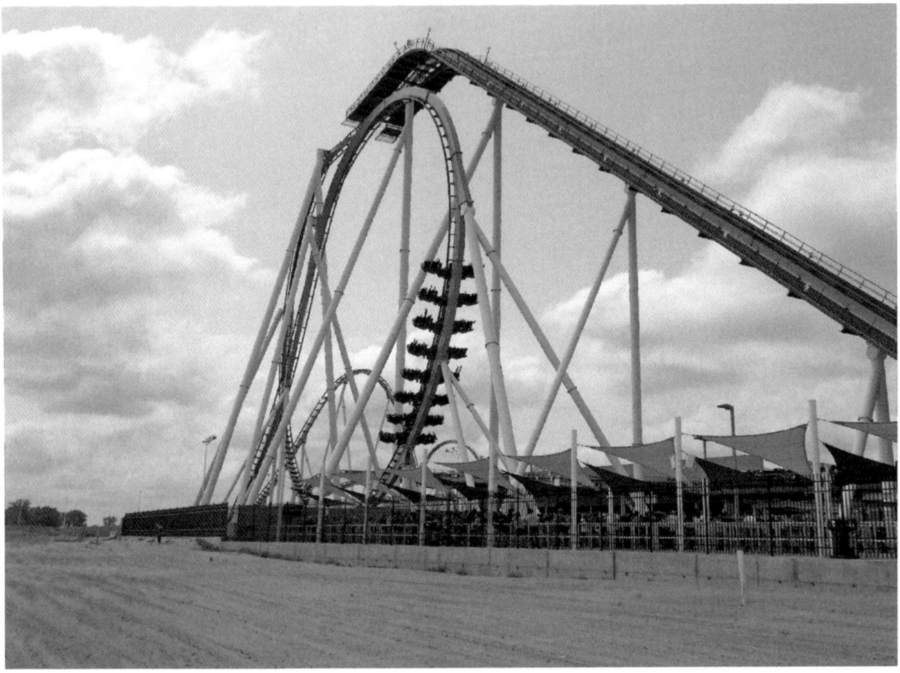

The Gatekeeper roller coaster was built where Lake Lab stood. *Photo by Kristina Smith.*

A. Boeckling, did not like that men and women who studied at the lab were housed in the same building, according to the Francises' book.

In 1918, the lab relocated to the fish hatchery at Put-in-Bay. It then moved to Gibraltar Island in 1925 and was renamed in honor of the father of the philanthropist who donated the island to OSU.

The Cedar Point lab was slated to be torn down in 1920, according to the *Star-Journal*. Today, the Gatekeeper roller coaster stands in the area where the Lake Laboratory was at Cedar Point.

## Hermitage House

When Cedar Point decided to expand its Funway in 1969, it demolished a structure that had housed the resort's police force during the winter, the *Cleveland Press* reported that year.

The sixteen-room Hermitage House, completed in 1905, was home to a small group of men who were the winter caretakers of Cedar Point.

There was no transportation or roads, leaving them essentially stranded in the structure. The group lived like hermits, so the Hermitage was a natural name for their home.

That wasn't its only use, though. Over the years, the Silver Dollar Café was housed there, and a dorm for employees was added to the home but later torn down, according to the newspaper.

From 1959 to 1963, the resort company's president at the time, George Roose, stayed at the home.

In its last days, the couple who operated Cedar Point's laundry service lived there, according to the *Press*.

## KaFraLu Island

Those headed to Cedar Point for a day of fun or a longer vacation usually get there by driving over part of the bay on a causeway that connects U.S. 6 in Sandusky to the peninsula.

The road stretches out over the water, and part of it was once an island that a family called home and turned into a summer resort for fishermen.

That is all that remains of what was once a small island that was the dream home of the Wagner family.

In the early 1900s, Louis Wagner and his family were living as squatters on the Cedar Point peninsula. Plans were in the works to develop the area into a resort, and they and all other squatters living on the peninsula were ordered to leave, the *Register* reported.

A boat trip gave Wagner the idea for his next home. He was cruising on the Sandusky Bay when his boat hit a sandbar made by the current off Cedar Point. He decided to turn the sandbar into an island and put his family's cottage there.

During the winter of 1908, the family dismantled its squatter cottage and carried the pieces on sleds over the ice from Cedar Point to the shore near the sandbar.

"The next spring, with the help of an uncle and some friends, we raised our house, rolled it onto a couple of scows and floated them with their cargo to the small rush-covered sandbar," Wagner's son Frank Wagner wrote in the *Register* in February 1959. "Here, the house was moved from the scows onto large wooden packing boxes. With a box under each of its four corners, the house now stood about four feet above the water."

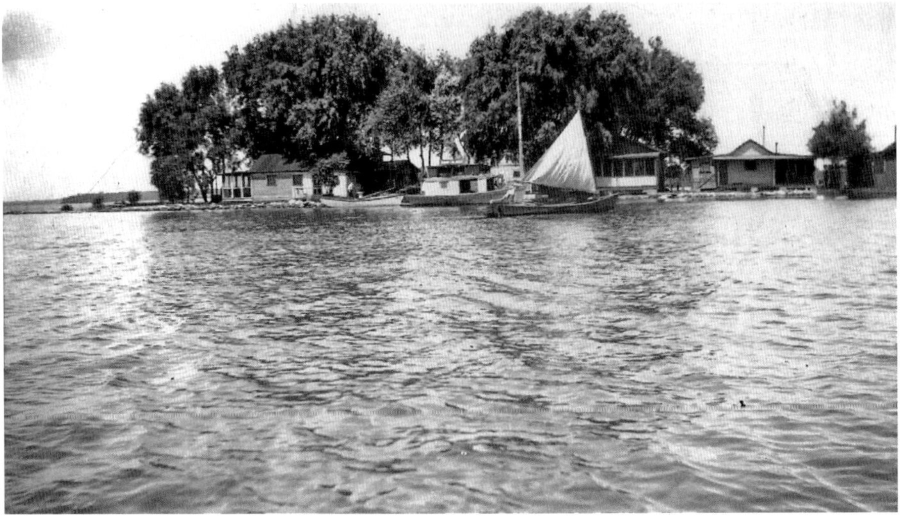

KaFraLu Island was a man-made island that became a family's dream home. It was incorporated into the Cedar Point causeway. *Rutherford B. Hayes Presidential Center/Charles Frohman Collection.*

The cottage measured sixteen feet by sixteen feet, and the family moored its motorboat to the porch. Rowboats went under the house.

Living there wasn't always ideal, Frank wrote. He remembered a bad storm during that first year that nearly caused his mother to abandon the house.

"It blew so hard from the west that she could not close the door, and the wind and rain blew in at the front door and out the back," he wrote. "When we arrived home that evening, she said that she was going back to Sandusky. Father finally coaxed her to stay."

Until then, the sandbar had been known as Sunken Island or Duck Island. The Wagners renamed it KaFraLu Island—Ka for Katherine, Louis's wife; Fra for Frank, the elder son; and Lu for Louis, the father and the younger son. KaFraLu was also the name of a boat the family owned before they built the sandbar into an island.

In 1910, the State of Ohio gave Louis squatter rights and declared the island his personal property. He started paying property taxes on the land.

The following winter, the family hired a man to haul stone over the frozen bay to build a breakwater for the island. The family collected logs and stones and used them to form a shoreline for the island. For twenty-five years, they continued to use those materials and waste from the Doerflinger Basket Factory to fill in the area and enlarge the island. The Wagners built six more cottages and rented them to vacationers and fishermen.

"Father was a great lover of flowers and trees," Frank wrote in the *Register*. "We had a dozen different varieties of willows, which he planted on our island, and they thrived exceptionally well because they were so near water."

The cottages were seasonal, although the family would visit them in the winter at times to check on the island.

"We would cut a hole in the ice to get water for cooking," Frank wrote. "There are many pleasant memories of the good sauerkraut and pork dinners we enjoyed on those visits."

The good times started to wane when Louis died in 1941. Gas was rationed during World War II, and it was difficult for people to get gas to boat to the island. The family found it more difficult to rent the cottages.

Then in 1946, a fire—whose cause was never determined—destroyed some of the cottages. The family sold the island in 1947, and the Cedar Point Bridge Company later took over ownership.

The Cedar Point Causeway was built over the island and finished in 1957. The causeway was a shorter route for cars to get to the park than the older Chausse, the first road to Cedar Point.

Although KaFraLu Island and its cottages are gone, Frank still recalled them with pride.

"When visitors to the island were astounded at what we had accomplished, we would frequently say to them: 'If it's work you like, then build your own island as our family did,'" he wrote in the *Register*.

6

# CEDAR POINT

## RIDES ARE LOST TO BIGGER, FASTER ONES

From a wooded fishing area to being routinely voted the best amusement park in the world, Cedar Point has changed drastically since the late 1800s. Today, it is the second-oldest continuously operating amusement park in North America.

Cedar Point is always looking to add taller, faster rides and new attractions to keep fresh entertainment for the millions who visit each year. The park has changed everything from its rides to how people get there.

Dips in the economy also spelled different phases of entertainment there, and though it might be hard to believe today, the park was on the verge of closing more than once.

The grand pavilion, which still stands at the amusement park today but has been renovated, was built in 1888 and included an auditorium and bowling alleys, according to *Ohio Cures*, a publication of the Lucas County/Maumee Valley Historical Society.

Then Cedar Point debuted its first roller coaster in 1892. The Switchback Railway was twenty-five feet tall and went ten miles per hour—a kiddie ride by today's standards, said Bryan Edwards, Cedar Point public relations manager. When the ride was over, the cars had to be manually hauled back to the top. Although it sounds archaic, roller coasters were a novelty at the time, and the Switchback Railway was considered a great ride, according to *Queen of American Watering Places*.

The coaster, bathing beach and other activities made Cedar Point a popular resort, and it had crowds sometimes larger than six thousand people.

Still, other resorts were popping up in the area, and they all competed to attract customers.

Put-in-Bay had the luxurious Hotel Victory, and in 1894, a resort was built on Johnson's Island, just across the bay within sight of Cedar Point and downtown Sandusky.

The Johnson's Island Pleasure Resort offered similar entertainment, and its steamboat service sailed from a dock near the pier Cedar Point's boat used. Some customers opted to go to Johnson's Island instead. By 1896, elevated competition from the island resort put Cedar Point into serious financial trouble. Fortunes for both resorts changed drastically the following year. A person was accidentally shot when a gun discharged during an event at the Johnson's Island resort, leading to a lawsuit. Before the lawsuit reached court, a fire destroyed the resort's pavilion. Those events were disastrous for the island resort and ultimately shut it down, according to *Queen of American Watering Places*.

That was also the year that Indiana businessman George A. Boeckling arrived in Sandusky and took an interest in the park. The Cedar Point Pleasure Company of Indiana was formed and bought Cedar Point, and Boeckling was its leader.

The details of how this happened appear to be lost to history, but Boeckling ended up bringing prosperity to the park and making it a forerunner to what we see today.

He built the first hotels and conceived the idea for the Hotel Breakers, which Cedar Point recently renovated. When the Breakers opened in 1905, it included amenities that were state of the art at the time. Each room had running water and a private bath, a rarity then. The hotel's design was inspired by chateaus Boeckling saw on a trip to France and was so upscale that impromptu opera performances were sometimes given in the rotunda during the 1910s and '20s, according to *A Summertime Tradition on Lake Erie*.

By 1920, Cedar Point was commonly marketed as the "Queen of American Watering Places" with "the finest bathing beach in the world," according to the resort's promotional materials from the era on file at the Rutherford B. Hayes Presidential Center. From beach attractions to thrill rides and roller coasters that faded away as technology advanced, Cedar Point made many changes to its attractions. Some beloved rides were taken out, sent to the junk pile or sometimes dismantled and taken to another park for a second life.

"When a ride gets older, its cost to keep it going goes up," Edwards said. "We've taken out some great rides, but we replace it hopefully with something better."

Cedar Point determines which rides should be removed by tracking how much each one is ridden. If one continues to have low or declining numbers, it likely will be the one that is replaced with the next big thing. Sometimes the new ride is taller and faster or a new family attraction. Park operators are always looking at how they can keep Cedar Point one of the most visited attractions in Ohio.

## Beach Rides and Amenities

By the early 1900s, the bathing beach had a water swing, a wooden water toboggan and a bathhouse that could accommodate thousands of people and rented out swimsuits. The boardwalk usually was packed with people, some of them riding around in wicker carts. Today, the beach continues to be a major draw, but the boardwalk and water rides are gone.

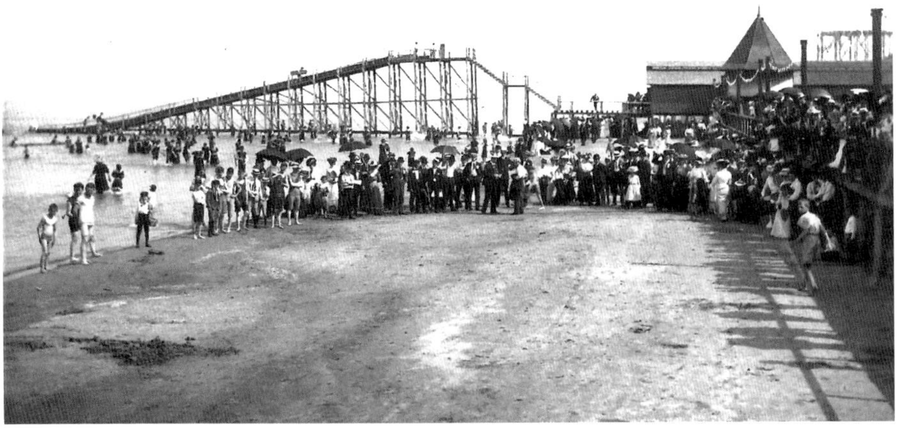

The water toboggan at the Cedar Point beach and the boardwalk were popular destinations in the early 1900s. *Rutherford B. Hayes Presidential Center/Charles Frohman Collection.*

## Eden Musee

The Eden Musee was an offshoot of New York's Eden Musee and featured wax figures that depicted famous yet gruesome figures and events, such as murders and executions. It opened in the late 1800s and remained at the park for more than sixty years.

"Never for the faint of heart, the terrifying scenes of the Eden Musee constantly drew large crowds," according to *Queen of American Watering Places*.

In the late 1950s, the company running Cedar Point began making major changes, and one of them was to begin buying rides and concession stands from their owners so the park could have more control over the midway and eventually charge one admission price instead of separate prices for each ride or attraction. The owner of the Musee at the time wouldn't sell. Instead, he removed all of the wax figures and left the building empty, according to *Queen of American Watering Places*.

The Centennial Theatre, now the Jack Aldrich Theatre, took its place, Edwards said.

## Crystal Rock Castle

In 1904, Crystal Rock Castle was built to sell beer, and it was named for the Crystal Rock beer brewed in Sandusky. The Kuebeler family owned the brewery, and one of the brewery's founders, Jacob Kuebeler, also was one of the founding partners of the resort's first managing company, the Cedar

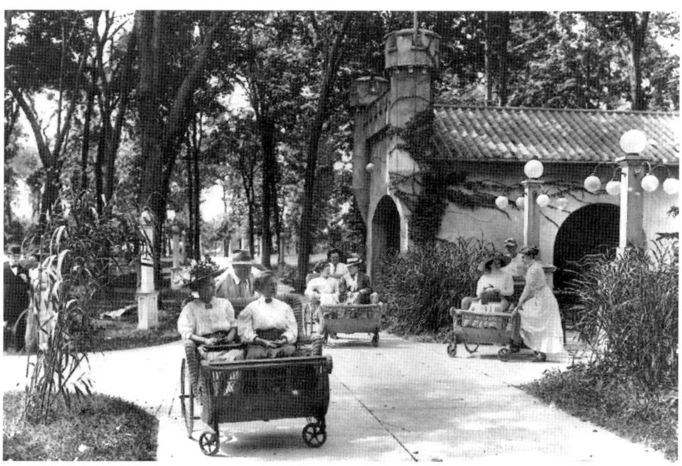

Crystal Rock Castle, behind these ladies seeing Cedar Point from wicker carts, was built in 1904 and served beer. *Rutherford B. Hayes Presidential Center/ Charles Frohman Collection.*

Point Pleasure Resort Company. The building's architecture incorporated turrets and gray stucco walls to give it a look of a stone castle, according to *Queen of American Watering Places*.

During Prohibition, which lasted from 1920 until it was repealed in 1933, Crystal Rock Castle was a sandwich shop.

By the late 1950s, the castle was closed and housed the park maintenance areas. At one time, it also held the resort's firehouse. The building no longer stands.

## Early Roller Coasters

Ten years after the Switchback Railway opened, Cedar Point got its first "big" coaster, the Racer, according to *Ohio Cures*. The ride was a figure-eight toboggan that went as high as forty-six feet. Riders could experience this thrill for five cents, according to *Queen of American Watering Places*.

The coaster was part of Cedar Point's first midway, which was added in 1906 to put the amusement portion of the resort in the same general area, according to *Ohio Cures*.

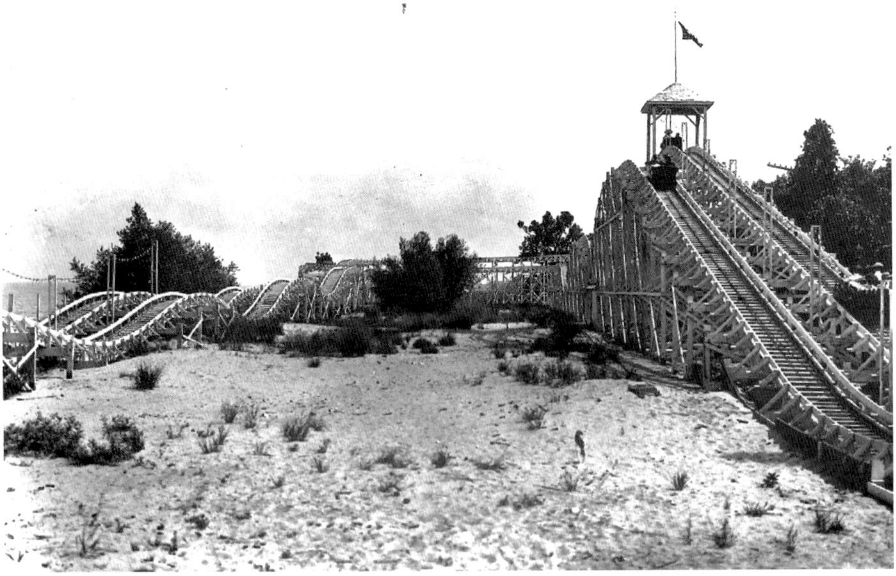

The Racer was Cedar Point's first big roller coaster. *Rutherford B. Hayes Presidential Center/ Charles Frohman Collection.*

Next came the Dip the Dips Scenic Railway in 1908, followed four years later by the even faster Leap the Dips. The Leap Frog Scenic Railway replaced Dip the Dips in 1918.

That year, Cedar Point had three roller coasters: Leap the Dips, Leap Frog Scenic Railway and the Racer.

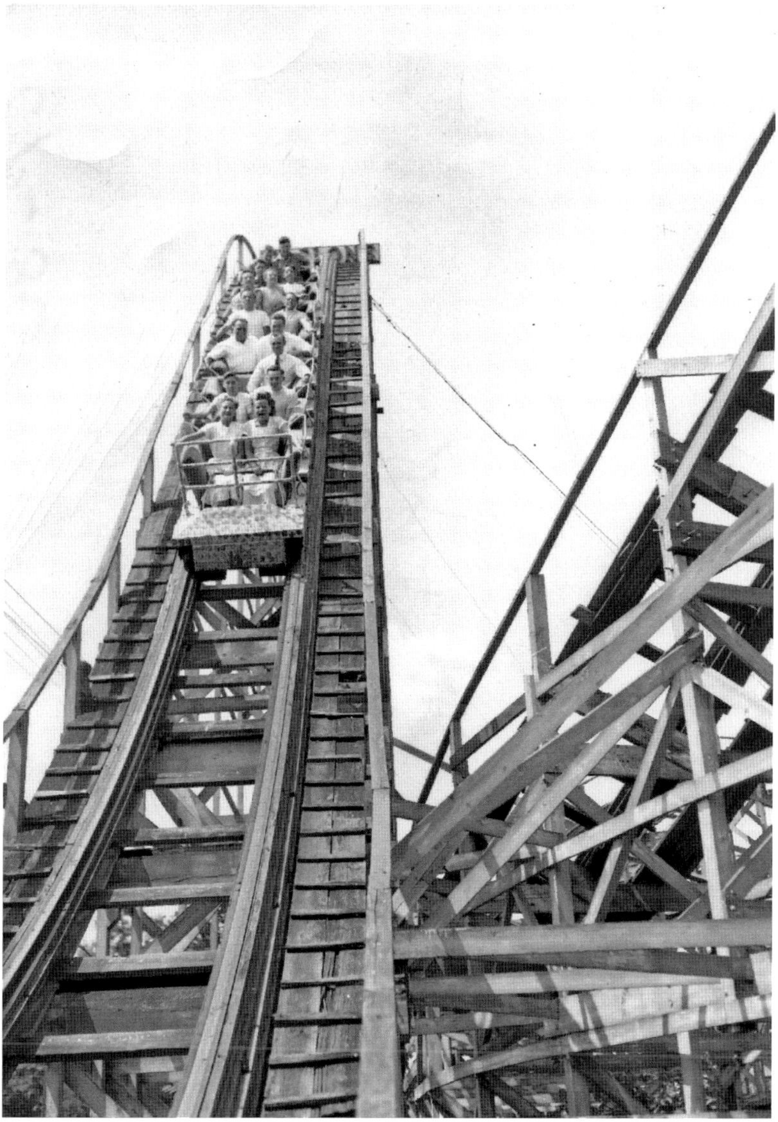

The Cyclone debuted in 1929 and lasted twenty years. *Sandusky Library Follett House Museum Archives.*

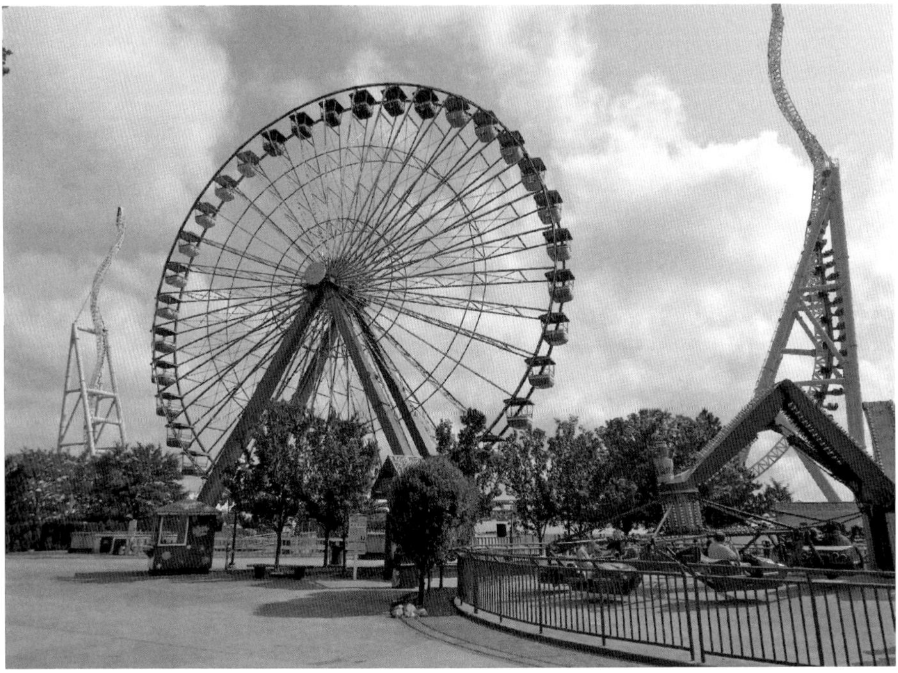

The Giant Wheel stands where the Cyclone was located. Behind the wheel is the Wicked Twister. *Photo by Kristina Smith.*

Leap the Dips and Leap Frog remained popular in the '20s but didn't survive the '30s, according to *Queen of American Watering Places*. Leap the Dips was a casualty of the Great Depression. It fell into disrepair, and there was no money to fix it. Leap the Dips was abandoned in 1935 and not replaced, according to *Ohio Cures*.

Leap Frog Scenic Railway was rebuilt in 1934 to include a seventy-foot hill and was renamed the High Frolics. The park stopped operating it in 1940.

In 1929, Cedar Point replaced the Racer with the Cyclone, a roller coaster "specifically built for speed," *Ohio Cures* reported.

"Steep Hills, sharply banked turns and spiraling turns and descents soon made the Cyclone a legend," according to *Queen of American Watering Places*.

The Cyclone would be the last big addition to Cedar Point for many years.

"It was a fabulous ride," David Francis told the *Toledo Blade* in 2002. "It probably bruised many ribs and broke a few bones."

The Great Depression struck in 1929, and Cedar Point was no exception to the devastation it caused. The company that owned the park paid its shareholders dividends in 1931. For decades after that, the park didn't make dividends to pay out, according to *A Summertime Tradition on Lake Erie*. It also was the year Boeckling, who had made the park such a success, died.

Money to keep up the park and repair the rides wasn't there, so although the park survived the Depression, it came out of it rather dilapidated.

## Steamships

In Cedar Point's early decades, steamship was the way to get there.

When Zistel built the first bathing house, considered the start of the peninsula's use as a resort, he operated the steamboat *Young Reindeer* from Sandusky to Cedar Point for twenty-five cents a ticket, according to *Queen of American Watering Places*.

The *RB Hayes*—named for the United States' nineteenth president, Rutherford B. Hayes of Fremont—began running in 1882 and remained a regular ferry through World War I. A variety of other steamers taking people from various parts of Sandusky and the surrounding area to Cedar Point also popped up.

Steamers also brought tourists from Cleveland; Detroit; Buffalo, New York; and Toledo to visit Cedar Point. Some travelers would come to Sandusky by train and catch a ferry from downtown to the peninsula.

Among the best known was the steamer *G.A. Boeckling* that began running in 1909, the *Lookout*, a publication of the Sandusky Power Squadron, reported in 1952. The red and white boat, built in Michigan, weighed 328 tons and could carry two thousand passengers.

The *G.A. Boeckling* took passengers from downtown Sandusky to Cedar Point for forty-two years, making its last trip on Labor Day 1951, according to the *Lookout*. By then, the ship had traveled more than 300,000 miles back and forth across the Sandusky Bay.

Constant maintenance made running the ship too costly, and cars were becoming the preferred way to get to the resort anyway. Three new motorized boats replaced the *G.A. Boeckling*, according to *Queen of American Watering Places*.

"Before new and larger rudders were placed to her hull, she was quite unmanageable in heavy wind, and it was not uncommon to see her half way to Johnson's Island, or if the wind were in another direction, near Big Island," the *Lookout* said of the boat. "Despite her faults, she was well-loved by citizens of Sandusky and of all 48 states who will feel her absence from her familiar position at the foot of Columbus Avenue."

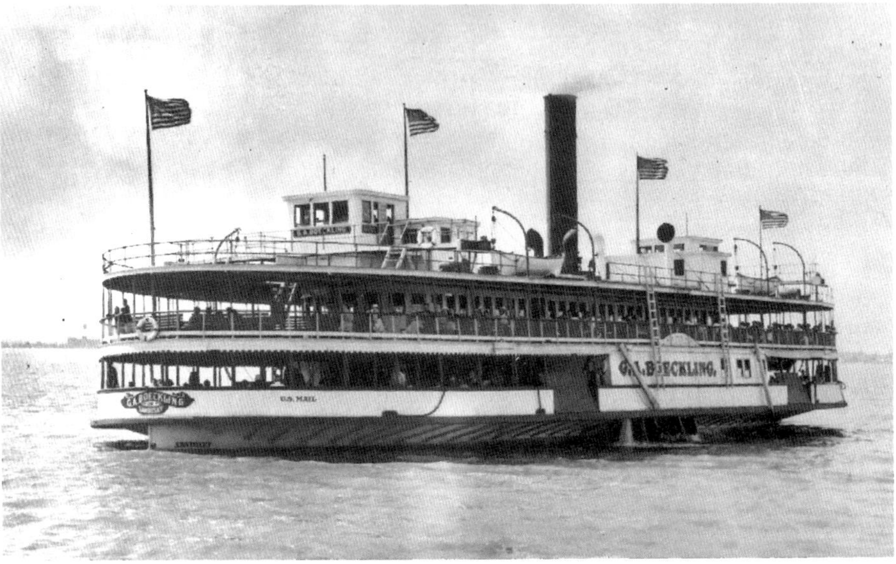

The *G.A. Boeckling* was one of the main steamships that took visitors to Cedar Point. *Rutherford B. Hayes Presidential Center/Charles Frohman Collection.*

A tugboat took the *G.A. Boeckling* in 1952 to Sturgeon Bay, Wisconsin, where it was turned into a waterfront storage building. In 1989, the boat was sent to Toledo for work, and a fundraising effort was underway to restore it. But a fire burned the ship beyond repair, ending any plans of its revival, according to *Queen of American Watering Places.*

## Big Band Performances at the Coliseum

Just as the park seemed to be pulling out of the Great Depression, World War II began. The Coliseum's dance hall would become the key that kept the park open.

The Coliseum opened in 1906, a grand behemoth that measures ninety thousand square feet and was reputed to have a capacity of ten thousand people, according to *Queen of American Watering Places.* The building, recognizable by its large domes, still stands, but its importance as a big-band performance site that helped Cedar Point through the Depression and war years is part of the past.

The second floor was a dance hall, and the first was a rathskeller, a German-style beer hall. A skating rink replaced the dance hall, but in 1939, Cedar Point wisely restored the dance area to take advantage of the big band era, according to *Queen of American Watering Places*. It was one of the largest dance halls in the United States, and it was considered an art deco showplace.

Everything from food to tires and gas was rationed during World War II, so the park was limited in what it could offer. The only remaining roller coaster was the Cyclone, according to *Ohio Cures*.

Cedar Point put its money into big band acts, sparing no expense. The move paid off. So popular were the shows that NBC broadcasted them live on more than one hundred of its affiliate stations, according to *Queen of American Watering Places*. Someone on either coast could hear the same performance that locals were dancing to in the romantic colored lights of the hall.

During that era, some of the acts included Benny Goodman and Glen Gray. After the war, the Coliseum remained a popular dance hall with big-name performers. Duke Ellington, Louis Armstrong, Guy Lombardo and Fats Domino were among the performers there.

The dance hall is still used for special occasions, Edwards said, but the days of regular performances and dancing are gone.

## More Modern Rides

Although the dance hall helped Cedar Point stay open during the war, the park still wasn't turning profits. By 1949, the G.A. Boeckling Company, which owned Cedar Point, was on the verge of bankruptcy. The park was put up for sale, but there were no takers. Instead it was leased for ten years to a hotel developer.

Meanwhile, the Cyclone had fallen into such disrepair that it had to be torn down. For the first time that century, Cedar Point had no roller coaster, according to *Ohio Cures*.

Smaller rides, including a Kiddieland area, were installed. Two businessmen, George Roose of Perrysburg and Emile Legros of Cleveland, gained control of the G.A. Boeckling Company. They decided that when the hotel developer's lease of the park ended in 1959, they would close Cedar Point and turn the peninsula into a housing development. The public was outraged.

"You'd have thought we had canceled Christmas," Roose told the *Blade* in 1970.

In 1956, Ohio governor Frank Lausche said that if the peninsula were developed into housing, the state would buy Cedar Point in the public's interest, according to *Ohio Cures*.

Roose and Legros abandoned their plans for housing and decided that they wanted to make the park into the "Disneyland of the Midwest." They spent 1957 and 1958 studying the park and determining how they could make some quick updates to make it better while working on their long-term plan. They poured $1.2 million into improving the park for the 1959 season.

They debuted the Monorail, a ride with cars that looked like pods and suspended riders nine feet above the midway, according to *Ohio Cures*.

"With its attractively landscaped entrance and futuristic appearance, the monorail produced more income than any other ride on the Midway in 1959," according to *Queen of American Watering Places*.

Attendance began soaring, and Cedar Point started turning a profit again, according to a letter the G.A. Boeckling Company sent its shareholders in February 1960.

Attendance increased from 760,000 people in 1958 to 1.25 million people in 1960, according to a 1961 letter the company sent shareholders. Then in 1965, more than 2 million people visited the park, the largest number in its history at that time, according to *A Summertime Tradition on Lake Erie*.

The Wild Mouse, which was a ride similar to a roller coaster, also opened. It and the Monorail lasted into the 1970s.

During this era, newer, more technologically advanced rides were added. The Mill Race opened in 1963, and it was the second flume ride in the world, according to *Ohio Cures*. Passengers rode in boats that resembled hollowed-out logs through flumes of water. Flume rides became trendy and were installed elsewhere after Cedar Point debuted the attraction, according to *Queen of American Watering Places*.

Mill Race remained at Cedar Point for thirty years. In 1994, the Raptor roller coaster replaced it, and the Raptor remains one of the park's most popular rides, Edwards said.

Cedar Point's oldest coaster is the Blue Streak, a wooden coaster painted light blue and named for Sandusky High School's mascot, opened in 1964. It remains open for rides.

The Western Cruise opened in the 1960s and lasted through the 2011 season. The ride took advantage of lagoons on the property, and the guides would give a running commentary as the boats passed displays of animals, pioneers, log cabins and American Indians who would "fire" at the boats.

"Passing a fort, simulated cannonballs caused geysers of water to erupt near the sides of the steel boats," according to *Queen of American Watering Places*.

Jeff Phillips of Lakeside worked the boats during the summer when he was twenty-one years old. He liked the creativity of telling stories to the passengers and that they seemed to enjoy the experience.

"[The boat] had a hood, so it was shaded," Phillips said. "I think it was a nice change from all the other rides."

The Western Cruise was removed to make way for the Dinosaurs Alive exhibit that opened in 2012, Edwards said.

Rides weren't the only popular form of entertainment. Jungle Larry's Safari Island opened in 1965 and featured tigers, monkeys, snakes and other exotic animals. The attraction remained popular for decades and stayed at Cedar Point until the end of the 1994 season. The owners also had an attraction in Florida and could no longer handle splitting time between both locations, according to *Queen of American Watering Places*.

The 1970s brought steel roller coasters. The Wild Cat and Jumbo Jet, which are no longer there, were built in 1970. The Corkscrew, a coaster that sends riders on 360-degree loops, is one of the coasters and rides that debuted during that decade and remains today.

## More Recent Lost Rides

Cedar Point has been home to the tallest and fastest roller coaster in the world a record four times with the Gemini added in 1978, Magnum in 1989, Millennium Force in 2000 and Top Thrill Dragster in 2003. Some of the more modern rides have gone away as those new coasters were built.

In 2009, the Demon Drop was dismantled and sent to Dorney Park and Wildwater Kingdom in Allentown, Pennsylvania, which is owned by Cedar Fair, the same company that owns Cedar Point, the *Port Clinton News Herald* reported. Installed in 1983, the Demon Drop is a 131-foot tower that carries people quickly to the top and then drops them in a 60-foot free fall to the bottom. It was operated 19 million times while at Cedar Point, according to the *News Herald*.

Ocean Motion, a ride that swings passengers back and forth in a giant boat, was moved to the Demon Drop's old location, Edwards said.

More recently, Cedar Point has focused on family-friendly attractions. For the 2014 season, it repainted the Jr. Gemini, a steel kiddie coaster, renamed

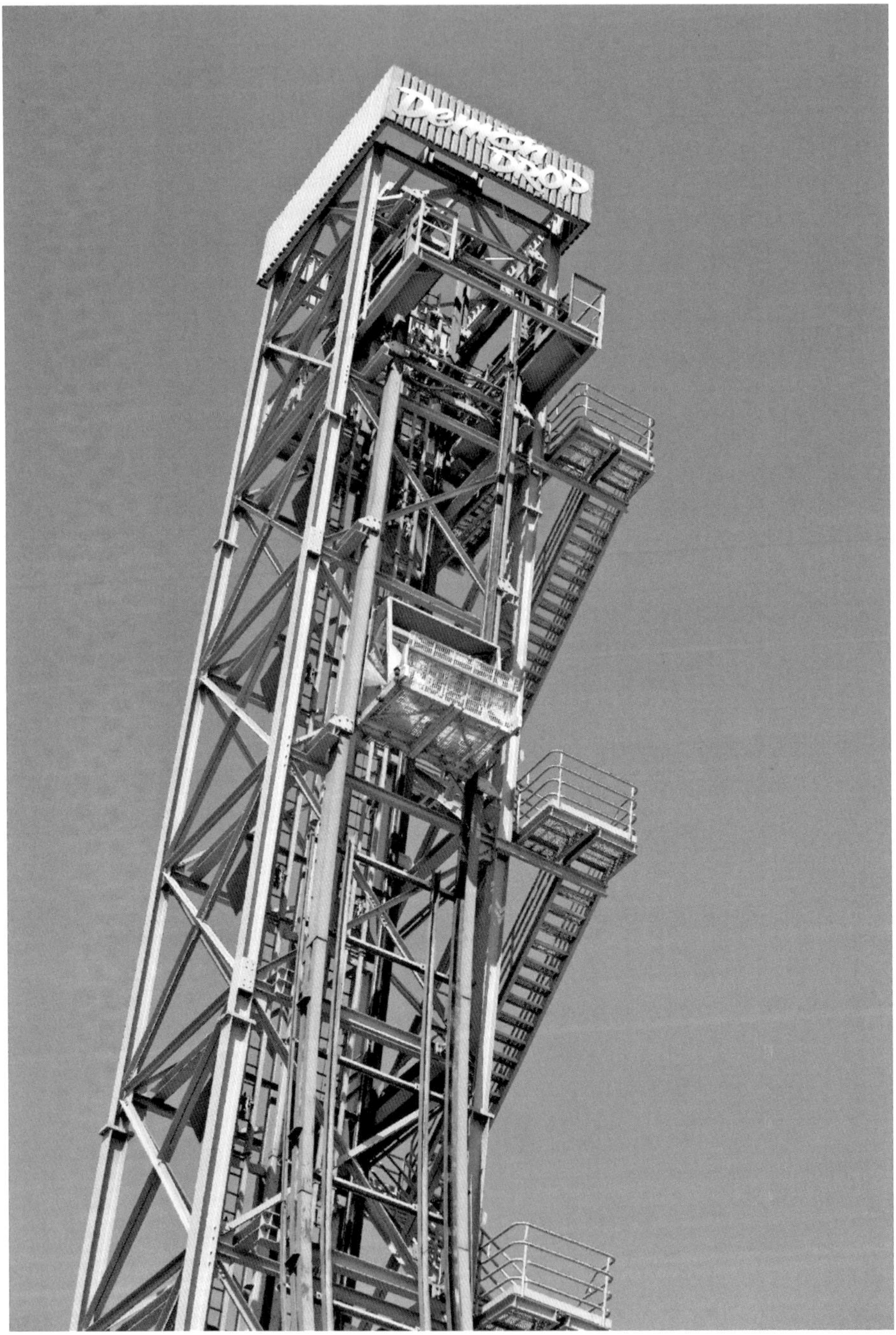


The Demon Drop debuted at Cedar Point in 1983 and was dismantled in 2009 and sent to an amusement park in Pennsylvania. *Photo courtesy of Cedar Point.*

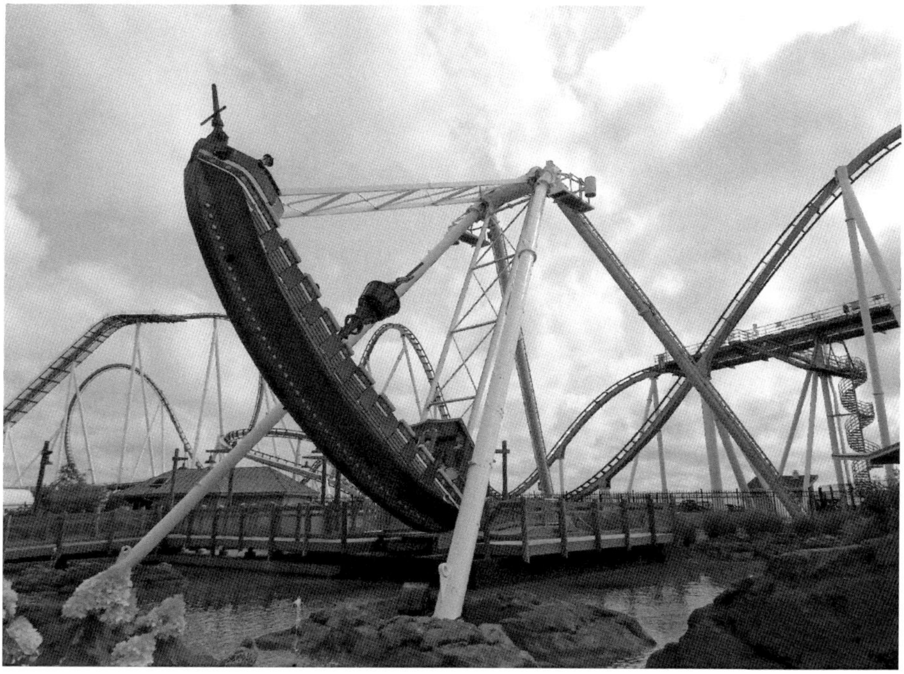

Ocean Motion, which swings passengers back and forth in a giant boat, was moved to Demon Drop's old location. *Photo by Kristina Smith.*

it the Wilderness Run and made it part of the children's section called Camp Snoopy, the *News Herald* reported.

The park also added the Pipe Scream, a combination of roller coaster and thrill ride, and a thrill ride called Lake Erie Eagles. Both are near Camp Snoopy and are family-oriented rides, Edwards said.

The 2014 season was the last for Mantis, a roller coaster where riders were standing in the trains instead of sitting. Mantis debuted in 1996, and at the time, it was considered the tallest, fastest and steepest coaster where riders stood in the world.

During its eighteen years at the park, Mantis gave more than 22 million rides. After the 2014 season, the park began revamping and repainting Mantis to turn it into a new coaster, the Rougarou, which was expected to open during the 2015 season.

The Rougarou is named for a werewolf-like creature from French folklore, according to the *News Herald*. Riders' feet will dangle from the cars as they ride on a twisting track at sixty miles per hour.

# 7
# TRANSPORTATION

Sandusky's role as a leader in industry and tourism also made it a pioneer in public transportation and shipping goods made in the city.

The city's location along Lake Erie's Sandusky Bay made it a prime stop for steamboat shipping and passenger boats.

Sandusky led the way for Ohio in the development of railroads when it opened the state's first railroad, the Mad River and Lake Erie Railroad. More railroads, including the Lake Shore and Michigan Southern Railway and the Baltimore and Ohio, sprang up around town, bringing freight and passengers. As a manufacturing center, Sandusky also produced boats and cars.

Dozens of steamships traveled the Sandusky Bay. Ships and trains brought settlers headed out west through Sandusky and dropped vacationers at local resorts. Boats and trains brought freight and commerce to the area.

After the car was invented, the city had nearly six car manufacturers at one time, according to the *Sandusky Register*. Today, Sandusky remains a heavily traveled area by boat, train and car. However, there are few passenger trains, and ferries have replaced steamships.

## Steamships

Some of the first means of travel in Sandusky were boats. At the foot of Columbus Avenue, steamships left Sandusky for Cedar Point, and boats docked around the city as they came from Buffalo, New York; Detroit; Toledo; and elsewhere.

The first steamer on Lake Erie was *Walk-in-the-Water*, according to the *Fire Lands Pioneer*. It was built in 1818 at Black Rock, New York, near Buffalo, according to an 1888 *Register* article.

The ship's first trip was on August 26 that year, according to the book *In the Wake of "Walk-in-the-Water"* by Gordon Wendt and published in 1984. It stopped in Venice on that voyage, the *Register* reported in 1860.

*Walk-in-the-Water* also stopped at Kelleys Island, known then as Cunningham's Island for the man reputed to be the first white settler there, according to the book *Lake Erie Islands: Sketches and Stories of the First Century after the Battle of Lake Erie*, published in 2004 by the Lake Erie Islands Historical Society and edited by Michael Gora. Kelleys Island didn't have proper docks, so the boat would anchor off shore, and islanders would bring red cedar on smaller boats to *Walk-in-the-Water* for the shipping trade, according to the book.

*Walk-in-the-Water* didn't have a long career. The ship wrecked in 1821 near Buffalo, New York, according to Wendt's book. But the ship was the first of many steamers bringing passengers and freight to Sandusky and the islands.

From its founding in 1818 through the mid-'20s, Sandusky was on the main route for steamship navigation from Buffalo to Detroit, Wendt wrote. Commerce on Lake Erie at that time was mostly geared toward moving pioneers and supplies westward toward the frontier. Items like flour, pork, whiskey and more were shipped by boat from Sandusky to the West, according to Wendt's book.

Steamers also brought vacationers to destinations like Cedar Point, Johnson's Island and Lakeside Chautauqua on the Marblehead Peninsula. Steamers like the *R.B. Hayes*, *A. Wherle Jr.*, *Chippewa* and others frequented the Sandusky Bay.

## Mad River and Lake Erie Railroad

In the early 1820s, canalboats were the up-and-coming means of travel. As plans for the Erie Canal to connect Ohio with the East Coast took shape, Ohioans wanted to have a canal section that connected Lake Erie at the top of the state to the Ohio River at the bottom.

Ohio legislators voted to build a canal in 1822, and they planned to have it run through the middle of the state to Lake Erie, most likely through

Sandusky, according to the magazine *Central Headlight*. But there was not enough water for this route to be feasible, according to the magazine.

So Cleveland was chosen over Sandusky as the site where the canal would connect the Ohio River from Portsmouth to Lake Erie, according to a 1947 *Register* article.

Losing the canal and the commerce it would have brought was a blow to Sandusky. Determined to keep their city growing, Sandusky leaders turned their interests to a newer form of transportation: railroads.

Sandusky's—and Ohio's—first railroad was the Mad River and Lake Erie Railroad, according to the book *History of the Western Reserve Vol. 1* by Harriet Taylor Upton. Ground was broken on September 17, 1835, and War of 1812 hero General William Henry Harrison—who would later become president and die of pneumonia after thirty-two days in office—drove in the first railroad spike during the ceremony at Water and Meigs Streets, the *Register* reported.

Upton quoted Jay Cooke, the banker who financed the Union's effort in the Civil War and who owned a summer home on Lake Erie's Gibraltar Island. Cooke's father, Eleutheros, obtained the charter for the railroad, according to Upton's book.

The railroad ran a sixteen-mile trip from Bellevue to Sandusky. Jay Cooke was at the groundbreaking, and he recalled the events during a speech he gave in 1900 at a meeting of the Firelands Historical Society, Upton wrote.

"But to my father and the Western Reserve belongs the honor of being the pioneer in railroad matters," Upton quoted Cooke as saying. "From this beginning, hundreds of thousands of miles of railroad have been constructed."

The Mad River and Lake Erie was the first chartered railroad west of the Allegheny Mountains, according to the Mad River and Nickel Plate Railroad Museum in Bellevue. The first engine was called "Sandusky," and it was the first to run west of the Alleghenies and have a steam whistle, according to Upton's book. It made its first scheduled trip on May 14, 1838, from the depot at the corner of Jackson and Water Streets in Sandusky, according to the *Register*.

The train had a locomotive, a small passenger car and a small freight car, according to the museum. The freight car had four wheels and an open top that was covered with a tarp in bad weather. The conductor collected passenger fares from an outside footboard.

Curling strap rails, called snakeheads, on the Mad River and Lake Erie were an issue.

"Often, they pierced the car floor to badly scare or to injure passengers," the *RFD News* reported.

If the crew spotted a snakehead in time, a train fireman often had to jump down and hammer it down to keep it from causing an accident, according to the newspaper. The trains must not have been moving very fast if the firemen were able to do this, the newspaper said.

Over the years, the Mad River and Lake Erie kept expanding and had lines to Springfield and Dayton, according to the museum. The company changed names several times as it joined other rail lines.

Eventually, Conrail took over the line. In 1998, Conrail divided it between Norfolk Southern and CSX Transportation, according to the museum.

## Lake Shore Electric Railway

One of the most prevalent ways to get around Ohio at the turn of the twentieth century was by electric railways, sometimes called interurbans. By 1908, Ohio had 2,800 miles of interurban routes, the *Toledo Blade* reported. That was 1,000 miles more than any other state.

In Sandusky, these lines began when brothers Charles A. Gilcher and William H. Gilcher formed Herdic Lines, a group of horse-drawn buses that offered service around the city in the early 1880s, according to the *Register*.

Next came electric trolleys and streetcars with different routes through the city and connecting with other cities. These were the forerunners of the electric railroad. One of the earliest interurban routes went from Sandusky to Norwalk and opened in 1893, according to the *Blade*. This line left the two-story depot at the Ohio Soldiers and Sailors Home—today known as the Ohio Veterans Home—in South Sandusky and was regarded as the second interurban line in the country, according to the book *Lake Shore Electric Railway* by Harry Christiansen, published in 1963.

Eventually, in northern Ohio, the Lake Shore Electric Railway took over many of these lines and linked them. The company was officially formed on September 24, 1901, according to the Fremont *News-Messenger* columnist Roy Wilhelm, a local history buff.

The railway went from Toledo to Cleveland and measured 116 miles. There were stops in Sandusky and nearby Bellevue, Fremont, Norwalk and other cities. The interurban meant many things to people across northern

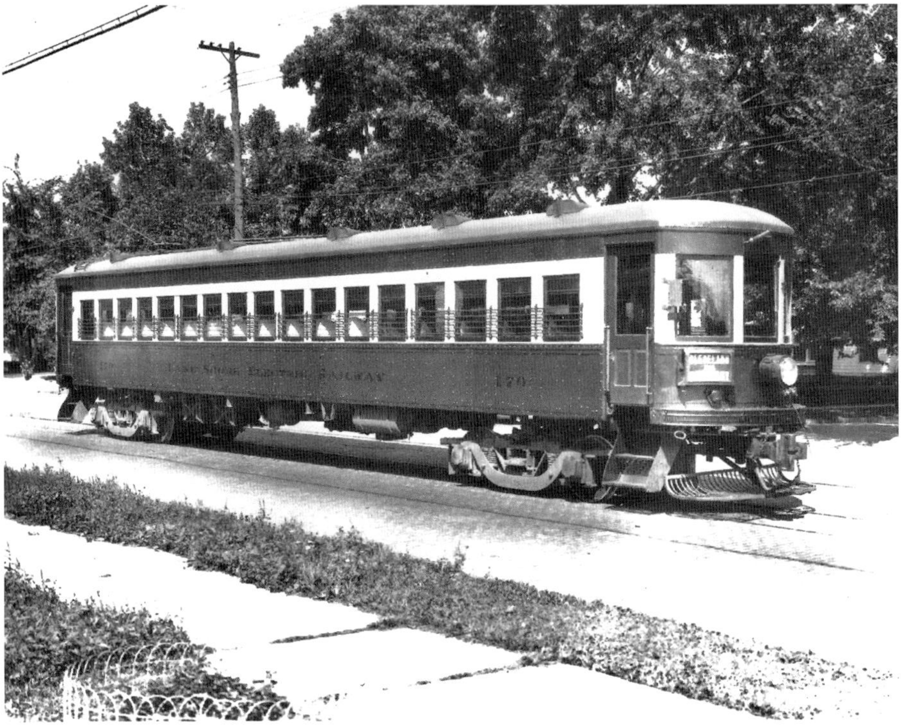

The Lake Shore Electric Railway stopped in communities across northern Ohio, including Sandusky. *Rutherford B. Hayes Presidential Center/Charles Frohman Collection.*

Ohio, who relaxed in the comfortable plush seats as they traveled to visit family or to get to work, Wilhelm wrote in 2014.

"It was transportation to school and home, to the store and back, to outings at the lake, and entertainment in the bigger cities," Wilhelm wrote. "It was the source of freight delivery for farmers and small businesspeople. It was a means of escape and discovery."

By 1927, the railway had 350 stops between Toledo and Cleveland, Wilhelm wrote in a 1999 column.

Automobiles, however, were growing in popularity, and rail business was beginning to decline. The Lake Shore Electric Railway was losing money when the Great Depression started in 1929, and by 1933, it was in receivership, according to Wilhelm's column. Service stopped on May 14, 1938, according to columns by Wilhelm and a *News-Messenger* article.

Some of the train cars, however, were saved and given some unusual uses. When a Fremont couple was remodeling their home in 2000, they found

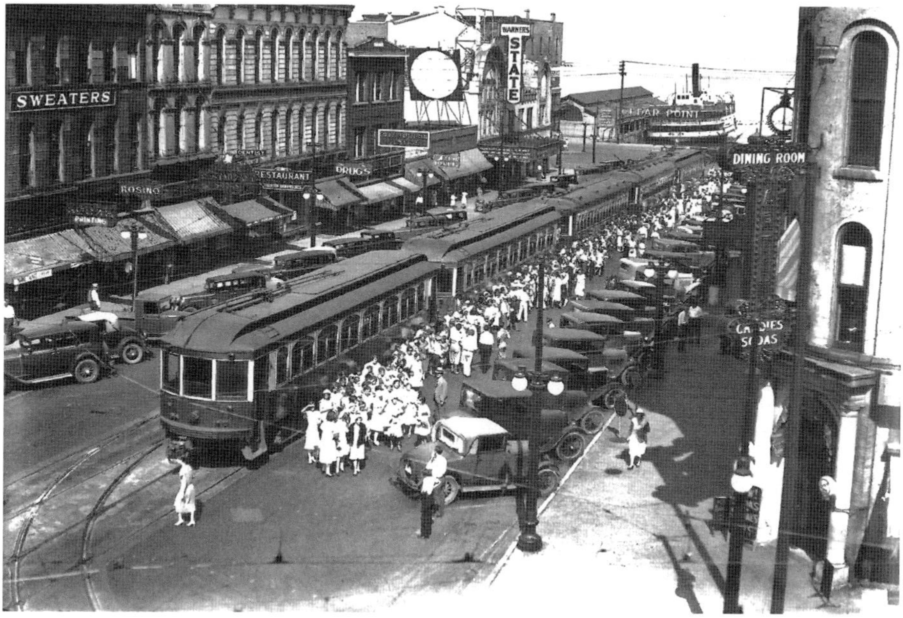


A 4-H group headed on an excursion to Kelleys Island stands by the Lake Shore Electric Railway on Columbus Avenue in 1931. The steamer *Chippewa* is seen in the background. *Rutherford B. Hayes Presidential Center/Charles Frohman Collection.*

the house was built around one of the Lake Shore Electric cars, the *News-Messenger* reported. As they peeled away a wall around it, they uncovered the words "Shore Railway" on the side of the car and realized what it was.

"It's not unusual," Fremont area historian Bob Lorenz told the *News-Messenger*. "When the line stopped operating in 1938, farmers and other people bought the cars for storage. Many of them were moved around."

In a 1999 column, Wilhelm recalled a spot near Huron, just east of Sandusky, where some of the rail cars had been turned into vacation cabins.

## Neuman Boat Line

The Neuman Boat Line was a ferry company started in 1907 by John P. Neuman, a designer and master builder of boats, according to a letter on file at the Sandusky Library Archives. He owned a boat works business in Sandusky, according to the book *The Beginning and Tales of the Lake Erie Islands* by Jessie A. Martin, published in 1990.

In 1911, Neuman built a fifty-foot gas-powered boat called the *Reliance*, according to Martin's book. It carried freight from Sandusky to the Lake Erie islands and also towed batches of live fish from the upper Sandusky Bay to the fish houses in Sandusky.

Neuman got into passenger service in 1921, when his boat yard built a sixty-five-foot wooden craft called *Messenger*. The boat took passengers to the islands during the spring and fall, when steamers weren't making those trips, according to Martin's book.

Neuman also took charter trips to the islands, Toledo and Detroit and towed a barge full of cars back and forth from the village of Put-in-Bay on South Bass Island, Martin wrote.

When John died in 1935, his son, Harold, took over the company and introduced the first double-end type of auto and passenger ferry to the Lake Erie islands. The boats allowed cars to drive on one end at the departure dock and drive off the other at the arrival dock.

At one time, the Neuman Boat Line offered service to Kelleys Island, Middle Bass Island, South Bass Island and North Bass Island, according to company brochures.

By the time it closed, it offered regular trips to Kelleys Island from a dock in Marblehead and some trips from Sandusky to North Bass Island that mostly served the island's vineyards, the *Blade* reported.

In September 2001, Neuman Boat Line treasurer Dan Newman told the *Blade* that the ferry company likely would be sold. The boat line did not reopen after that year. The company was a family business for its nearly one hundred years of operation.

"The Neuman Boat Line's been a tradition here for many decades, and it kind of marks the end of an era," Marblehead mayor Steve Plottner told the *Blade*.

A competing company, the Kelleys Island Ferry Boat Line, bought the Neuman Boat Line, the *Blade* reported in June 2002. The Kelleys Island Ferry Boat Line still offers service from Marblehead to Kelleys Island.

## Sandusky Automobile Manufacturing Company

The short-lived Sandusky Automobile Manufacturing Company opened in 1902 and was led by James J. Hinde, one of the founders of the Hinde and Dauch Paper Company. Hinde had the urge to build a "gasoline buggy," and he teamed up with William Muehlfeld of Eagle Carriage Company to make one, longtime Hinde associate L.D. Morton said in 1903, according to the *Register*.

This resulted in the Sandusky Automobile Manufacturing Company. The company made light runabout vehicles that carried two people and sold for about $700, the *Register* reported. The vehicles looked like motorized buggies.

In 1904, the company introduced the Courier, a slightly larger model. Hinde drove one of the Couriers from Cleveland to Sandusky in three and a half hours, a quick trip for a vehicle in that day, the *Register* reported.

The firm's vehicles were well received. In 1903, a representative from the English Motor Company stopped in Sandusky to look at the cars after seeing them at an auto show in New York, the *Register* reported. He talked about buying twenty-five to fifty of them to sell in London, but it's unknown whether he actually bought them, the newspaper reported.

Hinde's Courier model also attracted the attention of Henry Ford, and the pair developed a friendship after meeting at the Chicago Automobile Show, where Hinde's company showed the Courier model. Not long after the show, the company began making Couriers at its Camp Street location, the *Register* reported. Ford also visited Hinde, and the pair drove a Courier from Sandusky to the Thomas Edison home in Milan, according to the newspaper

"[A] number of cars were turned out," the *Register* quoted Morton as saying. "However, they were unable to get local support, and together with internal strife and the demands made on Hinde by the paper company, another of his enterprises, the venture failed."

The company was bankrupt in 1905 and closed, the *Register* reported. Hinde's friendship with Ford and his interest in machinery continued. After the company failed, Hinde went to Europe, where he bought a patent in England for a new type of engine, according to the newspaper.

When he returned home, he used the patent to begin developing a farm tractor. Ford tried to go into a tractor venture with Hinde, but negotiations failed. Ford Motor Company eventually got the patent for the transmission, the *Register* reported.

## Maibohm Motors Company

The Maibohm Motors Company was one of the larger car companies in Sandusky, according to the *Register*. Named after founder H.C. Maibohm, the company started in Racine, Wisconsin. After the company's plant burned down, Sanduskians brought the company to Sandusky by offering Maibohm $100,000, the newspaper reported. The company first had a temporary location and then moved to a building on West Monroe Street.

In 1919, Maibohm made 3,850 cars, which was a large number at that time, according to the *Register*. It concentrated on the B-6, a sleek car that could reach speeds of sixty miles per hour. An economic downturn the following year hurt the plant's production.

In 1922, Arrow Motors Company bought Maibohm, the *Register* reported. Arrow was backed by many of the same people who had backed Maibohm. Arrow changed the company's name to Courier Motors, bringing back the name Hinde had used in his company. Craftsmanship was the priority, and each car had a three- to five-hour test ride before it was shipped, according to the newspaper.

"If quality meant anything, the Courier would have been a resounding success," the newspaper said.

A 1923 advertisement for Courier's Brougham model touted the car's enclosed five-passenger cabin, windshield wipers, rearview mirror and trunk.

"Courier motor cars are individual," a 1922 ad read. "Each body is custom built in the Courier shops and has the brilliant, glistening finish associated with the finest custom painting.

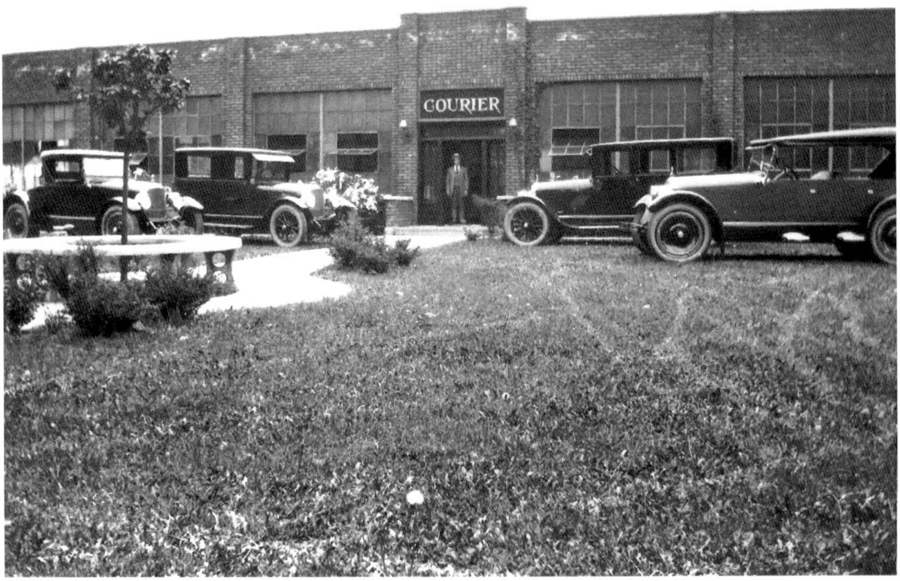


Arrow Motors Company bought Maibohm Motors Company in 1922 and changed the name to Courier. Production of Courier cars stopped in 1923. *Rutherford B. Hayes Presidential Center/Charles Frohman Collection.*

"You can always tell a Courier from an ordinary motor vehicle. There is a real distinction in owning a car that possesses its unquestioned beauty."

Sales, however, did not meet the company's expectations, and production stopped in 1923, according to the *Register*.

In a 1975 column, *Register* columnist Karl Kurtz recalled taking a Maibohm to Atlantic City with friends. When they made the trip, most roads out east were dirt roads. There were no hotels, and the friends slept in a tent until they arrived in Atlantic City, Kurtz said in his column.

"The Maibohm car had served us well, giving us no trouble whatsoever, proving at least to us, that it was well-built and engineered," Kurtz wrote.

## Eagle-Macomber Motor Car Company

Like his business partner in the Hinde and Dauch Paper Company, Jacob J. Dauch had an interest in cars. He worked with the Eagle-Macomber Motor Car Company to make cars and served for a time as president of Eagle-Macomber, the *Sandusky Star-Journal* reported in 1915.

Eagle-Macomber cars had an unusual rotary engine that was 75 percent lighter than other gas engines, according to the *Star-Journal*.

"Engineers and gas engine experts from all parts of the world have inspected the engine and predict that it will eventually supersede all other types of gas engines," the newspaper reported.

The cars, however, did not gain popularity as expected, and Eagle-Macomber went out of business.

## Barnes Manufacturing Company

In 1907, the Barnes Manufacturing Company made two types of cars: the Barnes and the Servitor, according to the book *Golden Wheels: The Story of the Automobiles Made in Cleveland and Northeastern Ohio, 1892–1932* by Richard Wagner. They were similar cars with four-cylinder engines. They were advertised as a "Gentleman's Roadster," a "desirable car for men of moderate means," according to Wagner's book.

The company, located at 1400 Columbus Avenue, showed the Servitor at the Cleveland Automobile Show in 1907, but it also discontinued the model after that year. The Barnes was made until 1910, according to *Golden Wheels*.

In 1910, the company was reorganized and renamed the Barnes Motor Company. It made the Anhut car, an open vehicle that seated two or four people and had been made in Detroit by the Anhut Motor Car Company, according to *Golden Wheels*. The company went out of business that year.

# 8

# SANDUSKY SPIRITS

## WINERIES AND BREWERIES

In 1842, Charles Carpenter moved to Kelleys Island and started what would become a thriving and important industry for the Sandusky area: wine. He brought seedlings of Catawba and Isabella strains of grapevines and planted them there, the *Sandusky Register* reported in 1947. Both, especially Catawba grapes, did well. So Carpenter started a winery there in 1852.

Settlers quickly realized the soil on the mainland was similar to that of Kelleys Island. Lake Erie's temperatures also sheltered the grapes from frost. Those conditions made Sandusky and the surrounding region one of three in the world where Catawba grapes could be grown, according to the *Register*.

"The particular chalk subsoil and limestone structure of this region plus the tempering influence of the lake bring to full maturity and impart to the Catawba grape a certain distinctive and delightful flavor," according to the *Register*.

Vineyards quickly sprang up throughout the area. The wine business became as important to Sandusky as other manufacturing industries, wrote Harriet Taylor Upton in the book *History of the Western Reserve Vol. 1* published in 1910.

"The luscious grapes which go into the city's score of wineries are raised to a great extent on the islands of the bay and in the vicinity of the city itself," Upton wrote. "It is so thoroughly a local industry that the traveler cannot but note the smallest land owner in Sandusky or vicinity hardly ever fails to plant his little patch of grape vines and contribute his part to the great whole."

Prohibition, which took effect in 1920 and lasted until 1933, hurt winemakers across the country, and those in Sandusky were no exception. But many stayed open by making sacramental wine for churches. When Prohibition ended, some of them quickly returned to business, the *Cleveland Plain Dealer* reported in 1935.

By 1939, Ohio ranked third in the United States in wine production, with more than 2 million gallons made each year, the *Register* reported. Nine wineries made the bulk of the wine, and six of them were in the Sandusky area.

Today, northern Ohio still is a winemaking region, but the wine business is not as extensive in the Sandusky area as it once was.

## M. Hommel Winery

Likely the best-known winery in the region was the M. Hommel Winery, started in 1878 by a winemaker who came from France to make wine for a company in the United States.

Founder Michael Hommel was born in Epernay, France, where Friar Dom Perignon accidentally discovered how to make champagne in 1688. Hommel learned the winemaking trade there, the *Register* reported in 1878. A St. Louis vintner sent scouts to France to find someone who would make wine with American grapes, and they found Hommel, who agreed and came to this country in the 1860s, according to *Sandusky's Third Dimension*, a book by historian Charles Frohman.

Meanwhile, a man who lost his land in Connecticut during the Revolutionary War was given land in Sandusky—part of the Firelands, where Connecticut deeded property in Ohio to people who lost their homes when the British burned their land during the war. That man, William H. Mills, moved to Sandusky and decided to use his property for grape growing. He opened a winery in 1857 just west of Sandusky.

When Mills tried the champagne Hommel was making for the St. Louis firm, he, too, wanted to make that type of champagne, according to a company history of the M. Hommel Winery on file at the Sandusky Library Archives. To entice Hommel to make champagne for Mills's company, he offered Hommel $1,800 a year for housing, an acre of land, a cow and a chicken. Hommel accepted, and his champagne won high awards at a Philadelphia competition in 1876. Mills was so pleased that he gave Hommel a gold watch worth $150, a large sum at that time, according to the company history.

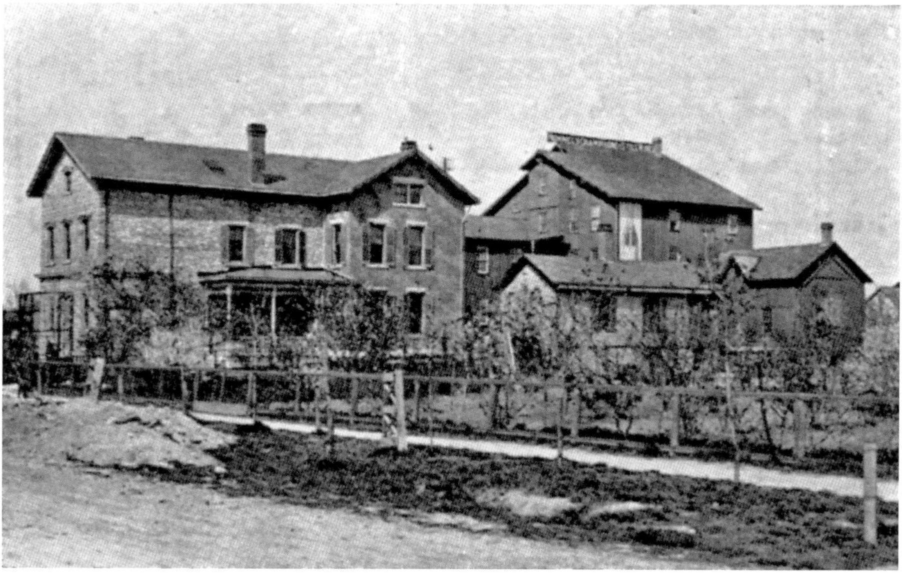

The M. Hommel Winery was one of many in the Sandusky area in the late 1800s and early 1900s. *Sandusky Library Follett House Museum Archives.*

In 1878, Hommel founded his own champagne cellar at 1422 Clinton Street, marking the beginning of the Hommel wine company. Hommel and his son, William Hommel, were the winery's top officers, and they took pride in their old-world processes of making a product highly in demand.

"It is Hommel's fine champagne, which requires three years in the making, that christens the nation's battle ships, and is used to open bridges, dedicate gigantic dams, and bring the proper festive touch to all types of huge, public enterprises," the *Register* reported in 1939.

In 1912, a bottle of the company's White Star champagne was broken across the bow of the USS *New York*, the navy's largest battleship at the time, according to the *Register*. Then in 1915, another bottle christened an even larger navy vessel, the USS *Arizona*, despite protests from the Woman's Christian Temperance Union, according to the newspaper.

Back in Sandusky, the company's limestone building was a popular destination, with its French garden and cellars that kept a constant temperature of about fifty degrees all year. That temperature was important to the champagne aging process, and by 1956, the cellars held about 1 million bottles of champagne, the *Register* reported that year. Over the years, the company's champagnes won award after award at various competitions.

"Old Mr. Hommel went to great lengths to demonstrate his pride in his champagne," the *New Yorker* wrote in 1960. "Nothing pleased him more than to entertain celebrities in his cellars, and for years, in the heyday of Hommel's, a steady stream of celebrities trooped down the stairs and wandered among the bottles."

Some of them carved their names into the casks. Among the famous guests were William F. Cody, more commonly known as Buffalo Bill, a bison hunter and army scout whose popular Wild West show traveled the world; conjoined twins Daisy and Violet Hilton, who were put on display around the country because of their condition; and bandleader and pianist Vincent Lopez.

A couple of sports celebrities stopped by as well: Notre Dame University quarterback Knute Rockne, who perfected the forward pass while working as a lifeguard at Cedar Point; Fritz Crisler, a football coach at the University of Michigan for whom Crisler Center basketball arena at UM is named; and boxers Johnny Kilbane and Bob Fitzsimmons, according to the *New Yorker*.

Michael Hommel died in 1903 after being kicked by a cow. The cause of death was peritonitis, an infection of a membrane that lines the abdominal

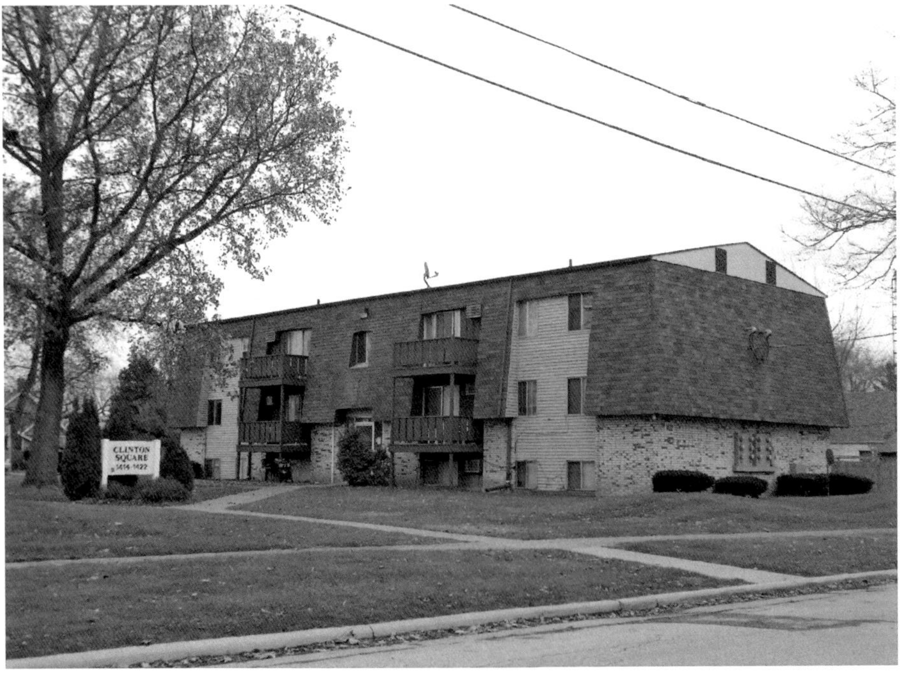


An apartment complex was built on the site of the M. Hommel Winery. *Photo by Kristina Smith.*

wall and covers organs in the abdomen. Peritonitis can be caused by the membrane being ruptured. His son, William, then led the company, and it remained in the family until 1945, when a Cleveland attorney's company took it over. The winery closed in 1967, the *Register* reported. At that time, it was the oldest winery in Ohio, according to the newspaper.

The building fell into disrepair and became a bit of a nuisance where youths liked to cause trouble, the *Register* reported in March 1971. It was slated to be torn down.

"The whole building is now a complete mess and a danger to anyone entering it, according to a police officer who investigated last night's complaint," the newspaper reported of a complaint that children were throwing bottles out of the building's windows.

A few days after the complaint, memorabilia and antique collectors went through the building and took any artifacts they could find from the winery's long-gone glory days. The next day, the building burned down in what authorities thought might have been arson. Today, an apartment complex is located on the site.

## Diamond Wine Company

The M. Hommel Winery and the Diamond Wine Company would be connected throughout the Diamond Wine Company's existence. Michael Hommel was a champagne maker for William H. Mills's winery, which would later become the Diamond Wine Company, until he started the M. Hommel Winery.

The Diamond Wine Company began in 1857 when Mills planted vineyards west of Sandusky. It was originally called Mills Champagne Cellars. The company was located on a high woody point overlooking the Sandusky Bay, according to the book *What: Souvenir of Sandusky, Ohio, and the Islands of Lake Erie* by Charles M. Hill and William F. Bolly, published in 1903. Ivy-covered buildings stood over the arched wine cellars.

The distance to Sandusky, however, created shipping issues, so the company moved into an old brewery building on the northeast corner of Harrison and Adams Streets. In 1894, Mills sold the winery to the Diamond Wine Company because of his age and declining health. The new company was a partnership of Mills's son, Judge Grayson Mills; the elder Mills's second cousin, H. Dell Cooke; and Frank J. Pelz, who had been the superintendent of Mills Champagne Cellars for seventeen years. The company got its name because its wines were as "pure, bright and sparkling as the old mine diamond," according to *What*.

Pelz managed the company until he died in 1902. A.F. Bricout took his place. Bricout was "known throughout France, Germany and the United States to be one of the best, if not the best and most successful champagne producer and wine expert in the business," Hill and Bolly wrote in their book. Diamond's board of directors at the time included Jacob and August Kuebeler, who ran one of the larger local breweries, and John G. Dorn, son of another local winemaker.

"The Diamond Wine Company is one of the strongest and most substantial concerns in this vicinity and destined for a great future, as the above names evidence and guarantee," Hill and Bolly wrote.

M. Hommel Winery bought the Diamond Wine Company in 1906, again connecting Diamond Wine with Hommel.

## House of Dorn

John Phillip Dorn was twenty-six when he emigrated from Germany to Cincinnati in 1828. There he worked with a vintner who was determined to make Ohio the center of the American wine business, according to the *Plain Dealer*.

Dorn moved his family to Sandusky in 1866 and brought some of the wine casks he used in Cincinnati with him. He founded the House of Dorn in 1869 at Franklin and Water Streets. Before it was a winery, the limestone building was a brewery, converted to a distillery and later used by Union troops as a telegraph office during the Civil War, according to *Ohio Tavern News* and the *Register*.

Delaware, Catawba, port and sherry were among the winery's offerings, according to company bottle labels. The winery was "noted for its superior sherry," the *Register* reported. During Prohibition, the winery gained a reputation as a maker of sacramental wines for churches, according to the newspaper.

The winery remained a family business. John Phillip Dorn passed the business to his son, John G. Dorn, who appears to have changed the company name at some point to John G. Dorn. The younger Dorn marketed himself as a grower and wholesale dealer of a complete line of grape and berry wines, the *Register* reported. John G. Dorn also gained a reputation in his later years as a collector of stamps and had amassed a valuable collection, according to his obituary in the *Register*.

He then passed the winery to his son, Richard Dorn. Like his father, Richard Dorn was a collector, but his interest was matchbooks.

"It is typical of the Dorn family that the business was never incorporated," according to *Ohio Tavern News*. "For three generations the Dorns, as individuals, have vinted and marketed Dorn wines. Family reputation is behind every bottle and family pride in every drop."

After Prohibition, the winery's business was booming again, and the operation expanded, according to the *Plain Dealer*.

"And we're going to have to expand a lot more," Richard Dorn told the newspaper. "Taking care of a demand that is increasing daily is getting to be a difficult matter."

A few decades later, business had slowed down. The winery could not compete with the lower prices of mass producers in California, and it went out of business in 1956, according to the *Register*.

The buildings were torn down in September 1970. During demolition, workers found foot-deep piles of Richard Dorn's matchbooks in storage areas around the winery office, the *Register* reported. An apartment complex was built on one of the winery's lots.

## Engels and Krudwig Wine Company

Lasting into the late 1950s, the Engels and Krudwig Wine Company at one time was the largest winery east of California, the *Sandusky Star-Journal* reported in 1938. Two German immigrants, Jacob Engels and Rudolph Krudwig, started the company in 1878.

Engels left Germany in 1848 to avoid the German revolution, according to the *Register*. In 1860, he planted a vineyard in Sandusky and later built a press house.

Krudwig first settled on Kelleys Island before moving to Sandusky. He joined Engels in 1878, and the pair formed the company. The winery was located at 510 Water Street in a building constructed of Sandusky limestone. A tunnel ran under Water Street from the winery to a bottling company across the street, according to the *Register*. The building also was close to the waterfront and railroad, and it took advantage of that to ship to nearly every state in the country, according to the *Star-Journal*.

"The stable antiquity of the vintage is reflected not only in the spacious cellars lined with great oaken casks, the old German pictures framed on the walls showing the feasts of Bacchus and other legends of the old German vineyards, but the business office as well is the same solid substantial old walnut that graced the early days of the business," the *Register* reported.

Unlike other wineries in Sandusky, Engels and Krudwig had its own cooperage plant to make and repair its casks, according to the *Star-Journal*. Even the cask hoops, made of steel, were produced at the cooperage plant.

Engels and Krudwig wines won awards at competitions in Paris and Chicago and gained a reputation well beyond Ohio for quality. The winery made sweet and dry wines, and some of its brands included Norton's Virginia Seedling, Sweet Catawba and Native Port.

"The sauterne wine produced by this company has for many years ranked with the finest products from Europe, and has won an international reputation for this city," the *Star-Journal* reported in 1938. "Recently, a French traveling man who had been served with a bottle of the sauterne thought so highly of the product that he made a special trip to see the plant where it was made."

During Prohibition, the winery made sacramental wine and grape juice. Its sacramental wines were so popular that religious organizations sent people to the winery to oversee the winemaking process, according to the *Register*.

After Prohibition, business picked up considerably, and Engels and Krudwig expanded its capacity from 500,000 gallons of wine to more than 1 million. The expansion provided "more jobs, more work, not only in the great winery but in a dozen contributory industries," the newspaper reported.

Generations of family members ran the winery, and it stayed open until 1958. The building was used as a mini-mall in 1970. Today, a warehouse is located on the site.

## Duroy and Haines

Captain M. Duroy and E.J. Haines opened the Duroy and Haines winery on August 1, 1888. They began with a wine cellar and fruit farm Duroy had in the area and moved to a brick building at 1636 Columbus Avenue in Sandusky in June 1890, according to the *Register*.

This winery was different from others in the area in that it almost exclusively supplied druggists with medicinal wines and tonics. The winery also made syrups with fruits for druggists and confectioners and flavors for soda fountains, the newspaper reported. Its products turned up in things like cough syrup and candies.

Duroy and Haines closed around 1915, according to Sandusky business directories from that time period.

## Steuk Wine Company

One of the smaller but well-known Sandusky wineries was Steuk Wine Company. William Leopold Steuk started the business in 1855 at the corner of Market and Decatur Streets. The building was both a home and the winery.

The family had lost money in failed business ventures and over the years sold groceries, often to the nearby Johnson's Island prison camp that held captured Confederates during the Civil War. Wine was a popular commodity, and the winery became the family's livelihood, according to the *Register*.

The Steuks had sixty acres of grapes in the area of Venice Road (where the village of Venice once was located) and in fields near Huron, according to the newspaper. When Prohibition took effect, the winery did not stay open, and the family operated a fruit market instead.

The winery reopened in 1948 at an old barn at 1001 Fremont Avenue. Then construction on major Highway Ohio 2 cut the family's vineyards in half, and the Steuks bought grapes from other growers to make their wines, according to the *Register*.

Sandusky barber and artist Elmer Grahl, who cut the hair of the winery's winemaker, Tim Parker, painted the pictures used on the Steuk wine bottles, according to the *Register*.

"For years, I was looking at his paintings and liking them," Parker told the newspaper. "We wanted to stay with something local for our labels, something relevant for the Lake Erie Islands region, and we thought, 'this might work.'"

The business operated as Steuk's Country Market, Winery and Gifts and was sold to four partners in 1993. It closed in 1997. The red barn still stands on the property, and a car sales lot and body shop are next to it.

## Breweries

Early Sandusky had a large population of German immigrants, and they brought the art of beer making to the city. Some locals started in-home "small beer" breweries that served homebrews but didn't have staying power, the *Register* reported in 1989. More businesslike breweries began popping up around the city in the late 1800s.

"Several brick breweries dotted the city's skyline," according to the *Register*. "The bales of barley and bushels of hops could be seen along large ice houses that were once packed solid. And every day, almost 20 teams of horses pulled wagons filled with barrels of beer to area taverns and beer gardens."

Two of these early breweries in Sandusky were the Phoenix Brewery, opened in 1851 by John C. Strobel, and the Sandusky Brewery, opened in 1852 by Philip Dauch, the newspaper reported.

## A. Ilg and Company

A. Ilg and Company started in 1852 as a brewery opened by Winson Fox, and it was later run by Strobel and Ilg, according to the *Register*.

In 1879, Anthony Ilg took over the brewery, located on Harrison Street, according to the newspaper. He also brought his son, Otto, into the business. The brewery put out about ten thousand barrels of beer yearly, and half of them were sold locally, the *Register* reported.

The brewery stayed open until 1890, when the Kuebeler Brewery took it over, according to Anthony Ilg's obituary published in the *Register* in July 1905.

## Kuebeler-Stang Brewery

German families trained in beer brewing ran two of the larger breweries in Sandusky: Kuebeler and Stang. They combined their businesses and later joined a larger group of breweries that were based in Cleveland.

The Stang Brewery started in 1890, when the Stang family bought the Sandusky Brewery on King Street by the Sandusky Bay and continued operations there, according to the *Register*. The brewery grew, and by 1891, horse-drawn wagons delivered beer throughout Sandusky and the local area, according to the book *Brewing Beer in the Buckeye State, Vol. 1* by Robert A. Musson.

On July 15, 1891, a fire ripped through the facility and destroyed it. Brewery owner Frank Stang, however, made plans to rebuild and had breweries in Toledo, Detroit and other cities fill the Stang Brewery's orders while it rebuilt, the *Register* reported in April 1893. The new building opened on April 12, 1893. It was five stories, and the *Register* described it as having a "commanding presence." Its location next to the railroad and bay made it a good spot for easy shipping by land or sea.

The Kuebeler Brewery was opened in 1867 by German immigrant Jacob Kuebeler and his brother, August, according to the *Register*. The Kuebeler Brewery was located on Tiffin Avenue in what is today an empty field across from the Industrial Nut Corporation, said Glenn C. Kuebeler, a descendant of the Kuebelers who has researched the family history. Jacob Kuebeler was one of the founding partners of the Cedar Point Pleasure Resort Company and brought the beer to the resort.

Fire heavily damaged—but did not destroy—the Kuebeler building in 1892. The blaze didn't hurt business, and the brothers expanded their operation to more than forty thousand barrels of beer in 1893, the *Register* reported. Like the Stang Brewery, the Kuebeler plant was located along the railroad and could easily receive ingredients and ship finished product.

"The hops are imported from Bohemia and possess that peculiar flavor which gives German made beer its superiority over all others," the *Register* reported.

The newspaper called the brewery one of the best in the state and said it could produce 100,000 barrels of beer a year, if necessary. Jacob Kuebeler was the president and handled much of the operations.

In 1896, the Stang and Kuebeler breweries joined together. Jacob Kuebeler became the president, and John Stang of the Stang Brewery was the vice-president and general manager, the *Register* reported.

The breweries made a variety of beer brands. The most popular were Crystal Rock beer, which was made with water from Crystal Rock Cave near Sandusky; Gold Bond beer; and Old Timers Ale, Glenn C. Kuebeler said.

In 1898, the Cleveland and Sandusky Brewing Company took over the Kuebeler-Stang Brewery, and the company continued to produce the popular beers. Jacob Kuebeler became a wealthy man, the richest in Sandusky, according to his obituary in the June 1, 1904 *Register*.

Prohibition, however, doomed the Kuebeler portion of the company, and it closed. The Stang Brewery, still run by John Stang, made soda and near beer, which were malt beverages that had less than half a percent of alcohol.

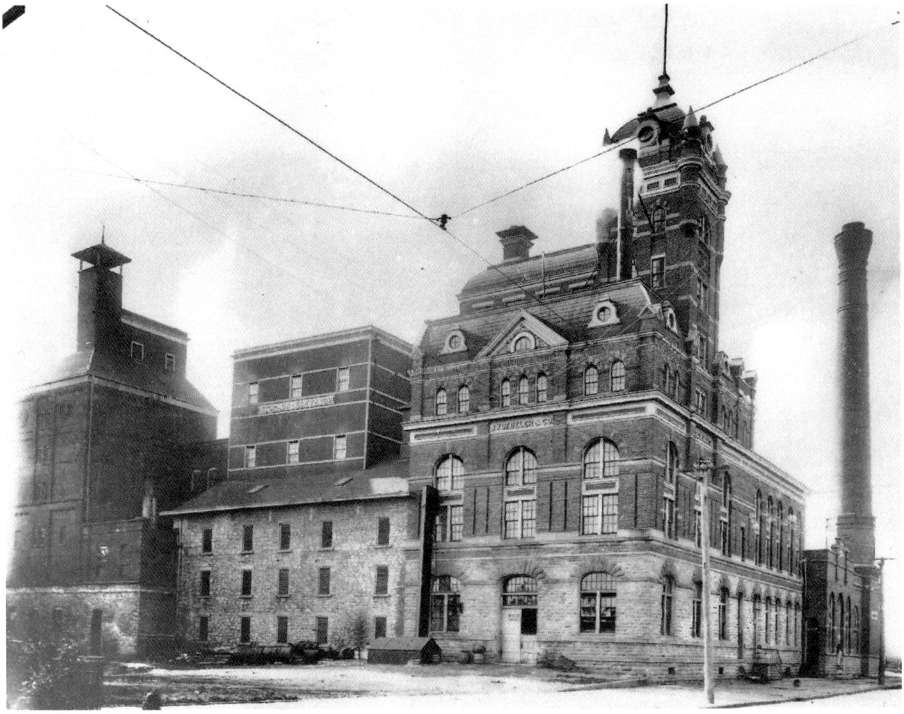

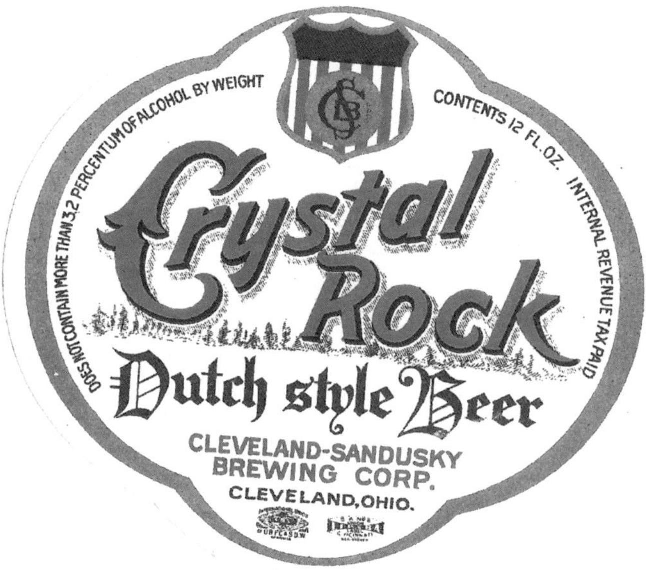


*Above*: The Kuebeler Brewery was located on Tiffin Avenue. It was torn down in 1929. *Photo courtesy of Glenn C. Kuebeler.*

*Left*: A beer label from Crystal Rock beer, one of the Kuebeler-Stang Brewery's more popular offerings. *Label courtesy of Glenn C. Kuebeler.*

In May 1919, Frank Stang was uncertain about the future but trying to be optimistic.

"We are hoping, however, that business will justify us in due time, in erecting a bottling plant and reopening the Kuebeler plant," he told the *Register*. "All depends on how our products are received."

The beverages kept the Stang Brewery afloat until Prohibition was repealed in 1933, but they were not popular enough for the company to reopen the Kuebeler Brewery. The Kuebeler Brewery was torn down in the fall of 1929.

"The wrecking hammers and acetylene torches in the hands of workmen have little respect for the sentiment that was etched in the once grand offices and brewing rooms," the *Register* reported on October 30, 1929.

After Prohibition, the Stang Brewery—still part of the Cleveland and Sandusky Brewing Company—again began making Crystal Rock and Gold Bond beers, according to Musson's book. A workers' strike in 1935 caused the company to close the Stang Brewery. When it was torn down in 1947, it was considered one of Sandusky's older buildings, according to the *Register*.

Although the brewery buildings are gone, August Kuebeler's home still stands near the old Kuebeler Brewery site on Tiffin Avenue. August Kuebeler's home, 1319 Tiffin Avenue, was sold to Erie County in 1947 and served at one time as a county detention home, according to the book *At Home in Early Sandusky* by Helen Hansen. Jacob Kuebeler's house was across the street at 1318 Tiffin Avenue. It was torn down in 1971, and a carryout occupies the site.

The current Erie County Juvenile Justice Center is down the street from the carryout, next to where the Kuebeler Brewery stood.

# 9
# THEATERS

As a center of travel and commerce, Sandusky had several theaters and halls with performances ranging from Shakespeare to vaudeville to entertain locals and those passing through on their way elsewhere.

The city became a center for the arts in the 1850s and 1860s and was headquarters for the national organization the Cosmopolitan Art and Literary Association, according to the book *A Pictorial History of the Western Reserve, 1796–1860* by Margaret Manor Butler, published in 1963. The group comprised people who bought the magazines *Harper's*, *Putnam's* and *Godey's*, according to the book. The organization used any profits to buy artwork.

Years later, moving pictures became the rage, and several movie theaters opened downtown. Notably, the State Theatre still stands today and is home to a variety of performances. Some of Sandusky's theaters and performance halls have been demolished, but they left their cultural imprint on the city.

## Norman Hall

Norman Hall was probably the first structure built in Sandusky primarily as a theater and concert hall, said Ron Davidson, Sandusky Library special collections librarian. The building was constructed in 1855 on Water Street.

The first floor was retail space, and the performance hall was upstairs, Davidson said. The hall was a showpiece of elaborate wood, plaster and fresco painting work with an impressive stage, the *Sandusky Register* reported.

"This hall promises to be the finest in this state," the newspaper said.

Through the years, Norman Hall played host to famous speakers, including abolitionist and well-known orator Frederick Douglass on March 16, 1864, during the Civil War. The *Register* reported on his lecture, titled "Mission of the War," on March 17, but the reporter didn't discuss what Douglass told the crowd.

"Neither time nor space will allow even a brief synopsis of the lecture," according to the newspaper. "Suffice it to say that it was a masterly effort—both as to matter and manner it was worthy of the speaker's reputation as one of the first orators in our country."

The theater also had a variety of performers, including little people like Tom Thumb, a boy who had stopped growing at twenty-five inches and was put on display by New York showman P.T. Barnum. An 1869 advertisement for a performance by Thumb, whose real name was Charles Stratton, boasted he and others like him would be at Norman Hall. They had just returned from Europe, "where they appeared before nearly all the kings, queens, emperors and nobility of the old world," according to the ad.

Hinde and Dauch Paper Company—which no longer exists—rented the building in 1897. The building and neighboring buildings then were incorporated into a five-story stone building, ending its days as a performance hall, according to Sandusky Library Archives.

## Biemiller's Opera House

Biemiller's Opera House was known by several names over the years, including Sandusky Opera House, Sandusky Theater, Grand Opera House and Nielsen Opera House.

Andrew Biemiller opened it as Biemiller Opera House in 1877, and it was located at Water and Jackson Streets. The upper floor of the building was the theater, and shops were located on the first floor, according to *Sandusky Area Sesquicentennial*, published in 1968.

An 1877 advertisement in the *New York Clipper* promoted the new opera house to have fifteen changes of scenery that were "all new with shifting machinery" and waterworks on the stage.

Over the years, the opera house attracted several actors who were famous in that era, including Edwin Booth in 1882, who performed Shakespeare's *Hamlet*.

Booth was the brother of actor John Wilkes Booth, who shot and killed President Abraham Lincoln during a performance at Ford's Theatre in Washington, D.C., just after the Civil War. Edwin Booth and John Wilkes Booth had opposing views on the war, and Edwin Booth supported Lincoln and the Union. Less than a year before John Wilkes Booth assassinated Lincoln, Edwin Booth saved Lincoln's son, Robert, from falling off a train platform and being killed. So Edwin Booth performing in Sandusky was very exciting for the city, especially because Hamlet was his signature role. The *Register* heaped praise on the actor.

"As 'Hamlet' he stands singly and alone—the one actor of the age who can play 'Hamlet' as it should be played, the one man who can give the full meaning and import to the sublime lines of Shakespeare," the newspaper reported in March 1882 after the performance. "Having seen Booth's 'Hamlet' no one wishes to see it played by anyone else."

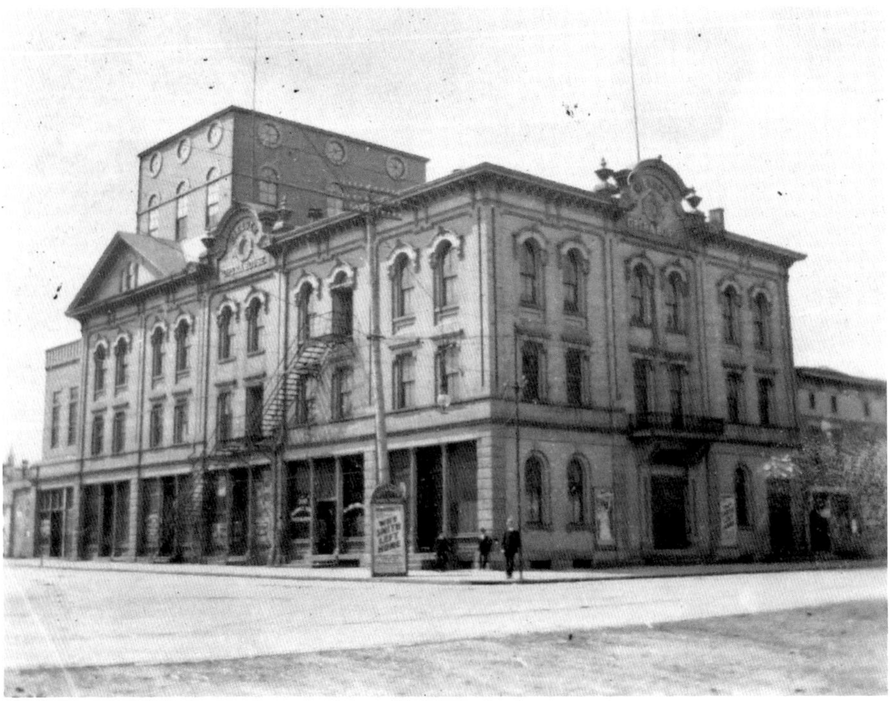

The Biemiller Opera House, also known as the Sandusky Opera House and Nielsen Opera House, was located at Water and Jackson Streets. It was torn down in 1955. *Sandusky Library Follett House Museum Archives.*

In 1895, Carl Nielsen took over the opera house, remodeled it and changed its name to the Nielsen Opera House. Seven years later, veteran Sandusky showman John Himmelein bought the theater. Himmelein made it into a modern playhouse with a ground floor and reopened it in September 1905, according to the sesquicentennial book. He called it the Grand Opera House.

"Because of the large stage and the location of our city between New York and Chicago, Sandusky became the famous stopover for a 'one-night' show," according to the book.

Productions ranged from comedies to tragedies and included *Rip Van Winkle*, *The Girl of the Golden West* and *Madame Butterfly*. A program for *Mikado* was printed on satin as a keepsake for visitors who saw the performance. Famous actors and actresses who performed there included Raymond Hitchcock, Ethel Barrymore, John and Lionel Barrymore and Maude Adams.

Himmelein leased the building a few times, and its name changed to the Sandusky Theater in 1908, according to the *Register*. The theater was sold to Seitz Amusement Company, which showed movies there. Seitz is a name that comes up often in Sandusky movie theater history. In 1951, the theater was for sale again and was facing an uncertain future, the *Register* reported.

"To those who can recall dazzling nights when the elite of the American stage answered curtain calls and those who are nostalgic and chagrined with the eclipse of the legitimate, it is a sad denouement," the newspaper reported.

The building was torn down in June 1955.

## Star Theater

The Star Theater was a movie theater that first was located on Market Street. It was a three-story building run by John Kessler, the *Register* reported on March 7, 1914.

Kessler got into a dispute with George J. Schade—a businessman and politician who was a city commissioner for fifteen years—over the theater property, according to the newspaper. Schade eventually got the building and erected what would be the Schade Theater there.

Kessler was not deterred. In 1914, he built a new theater building that would become the Star Theater on Columbus Avenue between Market and Water Streets, the *Register* reported. He rushed to complete the theater by May 10, and it opened as the largest movie theater in the city, the *Register* reported on May 9, 1914. It was also one of the most modern in the state, according to the newspaper.

The theater could seat four hundred people and was considered fireproof, the newspaper reported. It also had lighting, steam heat and four exits, considered a large number at that time and twice the number legally required.

"The front of the Star is of brick with a red field and gun metal headers, trimmed with terra cotta," the *Register* reported. "The lobby, in which 300 persons can find room at one time, is wainscoated [*sic*] with marble and white tile and has a tile floor."

Despite its beauty and modern facilities, business apparently was not going well enough for Kessler to pay his debts on the theater. In September 1916, a court petition was filed to have a receiver appointed because of the outstanding debt. William F. Seitz was appointed as the receiver, and he bought the theater in 1922, the *Register* reported in 1929. Seitz and theater co-owner Earl Seitz then sold it to unidentified "outside parties" in January 1929, according to the *Register*. Extensive renovations were planned, including installing sound for "talking pictures," and Earl Seitz was expected to remain manager, the newspaper reported.

But in October 1930, the *Register* announced that the theater would be closed.

By 1931, Warner Brothers owned the three remaining movie theaters in town, the newspaper reported. One of them was the State Theatre, which was run by the Seitzes before Warner Brothers took it over and is still in operation as a performance venue.

Over the years, the Star building has housed various businesses and is currently used as a coffee shop, Davidson said.

## Schade Theater

With Kessler's Star Theater moved to Columbus Avenue, Schade was free to build his theater on Market Street. On March 7, 1914, the *Register* reported Schade's plans to build a two-story theater in the Star's place. Those plans were put on hold for months, but in December 1914, Schade told the newspaper he still planned to build the theater.

His theater would be located on the space occupied at that time by the Alhambra Theater and Bogert jewelry store, according to the newspaper. It's not clear whether those establishments were in the same spot as the first Star or whether Schade moved his project to another Market Street lot.

Regardless, Schade built his theater and opened it on December 19, 1915, according to the *Register*. Films were shown in the old theater the night before the opening, and the old theater was expected to be demolished on December 20, according to the newspaper.

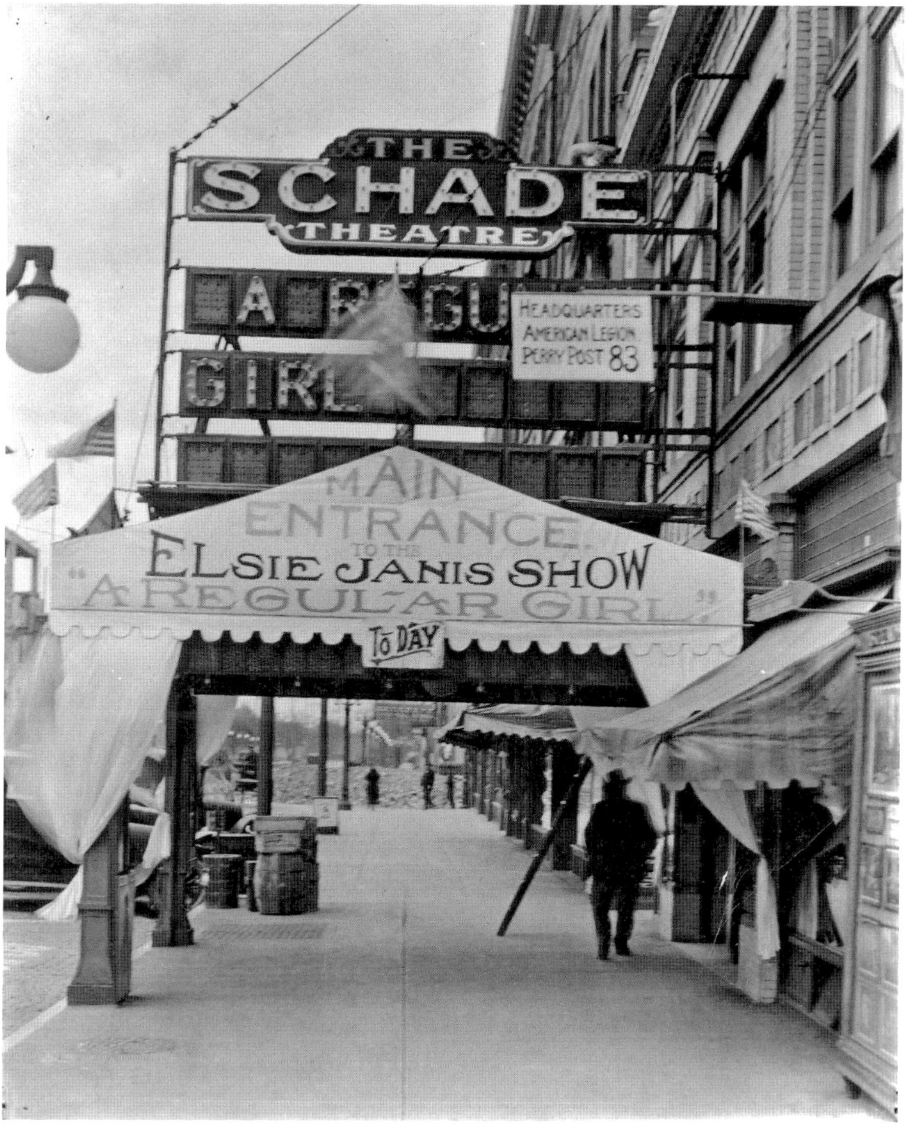


The Schade Theater advertises its showing of the movie *A Regular Girl* in May 1920. *Sandusky Library Follett House Museum Archives.*

"Nothing that money could provide has been left undone by George J. Schade, the owner, to make the new movie house one of the most beautiful in the state," the newspaper reported on opening day.

The *Register* referred to the theater as the "new Alhambra." Davidson said the theater apparently first was called Schade's Alhambra, but the name was later changed to Schade Theater.

Schade died in March 1931. Around 1930 or 1932, Warner Brothers acquired the theater and changed it to Warner's Ohio, Davidson said.

More than forty years later, the theater had changed hands again. And its proprietors started showing movies that drew the public's ire.

The theater was renamed Ohio Adult Cinema and opened in 1979 to show pornographic movies, according to the *Register*.

Within the first week the adult theater was open, the Sandusky City Commission called for it to be shut down. Local law enforcement obtained search warrants, raided the business and seized movies. Police charged three employees with pandering obscenity, the *Register* reported.

At the time, there were few theater customers, and Captain Curt Muehling of the Sandusky Police Department told the *Register* that there were probably more undercover police officers there than actual patrons. Then an electrical fire shut down the theater for a little more than a month.

Management was not deterred and reopened. In November, the cases against two of the three employees were dismissed, and the third received a fine and suspended jail sentence. The theater was back in business.

Also undeterred, the pastor of a local church led teenagers to picket the theater and pass out fliers protesting the pornographic movies, the *Register* reported. Police weren't giving up either. They raided the theater again in January 1980, took movies and projectors and again charged two employees with pandering.

In March, a judge ruled that the theater could not have its projectors back because it didn't prove who actually owned the equipment, according to the newspaper. So the employees bought new projectors and went back to work.

The following month, the two employees stood trial, and a jury found them guilty of pandering, the newspaper reported. They were fined $1,000 each and had to serve a day in jail. This apparently was enough for the operators of Ohio Adult Cinema, and they shut down the business. The building was torn down in 1985, and the land became a parking lot.

## Sandusky Drive-in

Earl Seitz built the Sandusky Drive-in in 1949, according to the *Register*. The theater held five hundred cars and covered ten and a half acres of land at 3711 Cleveland Road.

The theater was a destination for families to have an inexpensive evening of entertainment, where they could watch multiple movies and indulge in the snack bar, according to the newspaper.

The theater was open during the summer seasons. Business began to dwindle around 1991, and the theater did not reopen after the 2001 season, according to the newspaper.

"The theater wasn't kept up right," Steve Megyesi, who worked for 27 years as a projectionist at the theater, told the *Register* in 2002. "The theater needed to be repainted and cleaned, and the snack bar was taken away 10 years ago."

The last major improvements to the theater were new projector heads installed in 1970, according to the newspaper. The land was made part of the East Sandusky Bay MetroPark.

*10*

# A LOST SHOPPING EXPERIENCE

In Sandusky, commerce revolved around the downtown, near the docks and railroad tracks where steamers and railroads brought supplies and passengers.

As the city grew and times changed in the twentieth century, downtown still remained the place to shop, with department stores such as J.C. Penney and five-and-dime stores, including S.S. Kresge, often found in many communities. LaSalle department store, which was part of the J.H. Macy Company, and F.W. Woolworth also had locations in downtown Sandusky.

There were also shoe stores and a drugstore with a soda fountain, locals who grew up in Sandusky recalled. They have fond memories of shopping at the stores and getting milkshakes at downtown lunch counters. In the evenings, they would "buzz the avenue," or cruise through downtown and meet up with other friends, said Mike Marsinko, fifty-seven, who grew up in Sandusky.

"You had to have a cool car," he said. "That was fun."

By the 1980s, shopping malls and strip malls were becoming more popular, and stores moved away from downtowns. Changing times and fashions also caused stores to leave as people started buying more jeans and casual clothes than dress clothes. Big-box stores popularized in the late twentieth century also took business away from small stores around the country.

Sandusky, like so many cities across the country, lost downtown stores to these factors. And some of the once popular shops became obsolete and disappeared.

Today, the downtown has plenty of popular restaurants and specialty stores, but the day of downtown department stores is mostly gone.

## Millineries

In the early 1900s, a woman's ensemble wasn't complete without a hat. Trips to church, shopping or dinner were always hat-worthy occasions. These weren't the knit hats or baseball caps seen so often today. Hats were adorned with feathers, ribbons, flowers and pins. They were works of art.

Women of Sandusky were in tune with the fashion of the day, and there were plenty of hat shops, called millineries, to cater to them. One of them was Bamberger's Hat Shop, located in 1914 at 162 Columbus Avenue. It then moved in 1934 to the first floor of the Hotel Rieger on West Market Street. The proprietors in 1934 were Alice and Jacob Bamberger, according to an advertisement in the *Sandusky Register*.

In 1913, the number of millineries in Sandusky peaked, wrote Follett House Museum historians Virginia Steinemann and Helen Hansen in the "Follett House Scrapbook," a regular historical feature the pair wrote for the *Register*. The shops included the Lena Ahrens store on Camp Street, Tina Schwenk Millinery on West Washington Street, P & Fox Company on Hancock Street, Gilcher-Wallen on Hancock Street and Mary Godfrey's millinery downtown.

Yvonne Fievet worked in some of the millineries before opening her own. Steinemann and Hansen interviewed her in 1989, when she was ninety-eight. She recalled making the hats with a coarse cloth, called buckram, and wire edging. She then would cover these bases with silk, velvet or lace and add decorations.

Easter was the biggest time of year for millineries. Women often wanted a special hat for the holiday. As the popularity of wearing hats for most occasions declined over the years, women still liked to wear hats on Easter.

By 1955, there were four millineries left, and one of them was Fievet's shop, according to the "Follett House Scrapbook." Eventually, they all closed.

Then in 1996, a father and son opened a specialty hat store for women called the Revelations Store, on West Market Street, to cater to women who still wanted a fashionable dress hat. The store closed in 2001.

## Manhattan Clothing Store

The Manhattan Clothing Store opened in 1895 at a storefront on West Market Street, according to the *Register*.

Around the early 1960s, the store moved to 238 Columbus Avenue, where it remained until it closed in 1983. Shoppers were moving away from downtown. The store's branch in Tiffin was showing more promise, and the company decided to focus on that location, according to the newspaper.

In early 2015, the Sandusky storefront that once housed the Manhattan Clothing Store was empty, and the building was for sale.

## Weber's Fine Fashions

In 1938, Sam and Mildred Weber opened Weber's Fine Fashions at 129 Market Street.

Over the years, the store sold menswear and women's clothing and changed names a few times, the *Register* reported. It was known as Weber's Smart Men's Wear and Ladies Manish Tailored Suits and Coats in 1946 and Weber's Smart Men's Wear and Furnishings in 1950, according to the newspaper.

"Weber's always had extra fine suits," Marsinko said.

The store expanded and opened Weber's Tuxedo Shop at 125 Market Street in 1992, the *Register* reported.

But Internet and catalogue shopping and the development of shopping centers outside downtown cut into business, and the store closed in 2000, according to the newspaper. Three generations of the Weber family ran the store. The last was the founders' grandson, Dennis Hahn.

Today, the restaurant J. Bistro is located where Weber's was.

## Holzaepfel's Sports and Photo Center

Brothers Carl and Norman Holzaepfel founded Holzaepfel Brothers, a news agency, around the turn of the twentieth century at a home in Sandusky, according to the publication *Monthly Bulletin of Erie County Employment Service*. Two years later, they had a sporting goods store at 119 Columbus Avenue, where they also sold novelties, cigars and tobacco.

By 1918, the store featured photo supplies and sporting goods and was known as the "Kodak Store," the publication reported. After World War II, the store moved to 157 Columbus Avenue and continued to sell sporting goods but added clothes, such as bathing suits and sweaters, and pet supplies, such as dog harnesses. The company also opened a branch store in nearby Lakeside and at some point ran a summer clothing shop at the Breakers Hotel at Cedar Point, according to the publication.

In 1984, the business was known as Holzaepfel's Sports and Photo Center, and it moved out of its last downtown location—162 Columbus Avenue—to the Perkins Plaza. The store sold sports uniforms, trophies and other gear, according to the Sandusky business directory published that year.

Holzaepfel's closed in 1985.

## Caryl Crane

Caryl Crane was a women's clothing store named after a Sandusky woman who was a Broadway singer. Caryl Crane's given name was Fannie Shiff, but she changed it when she went to New York, according to the *Register*. Her voice coach felt she needed a stage name, and after that, she was known as Caryl Crane, she told the newspaper. She sang in musicals and on the radio before coming back to Sandusky.

She and her brother, B. Robert Shiff, opened the Caryl Crane store in the late 1940s on Columbus Avenue. The shop was in a storefront between

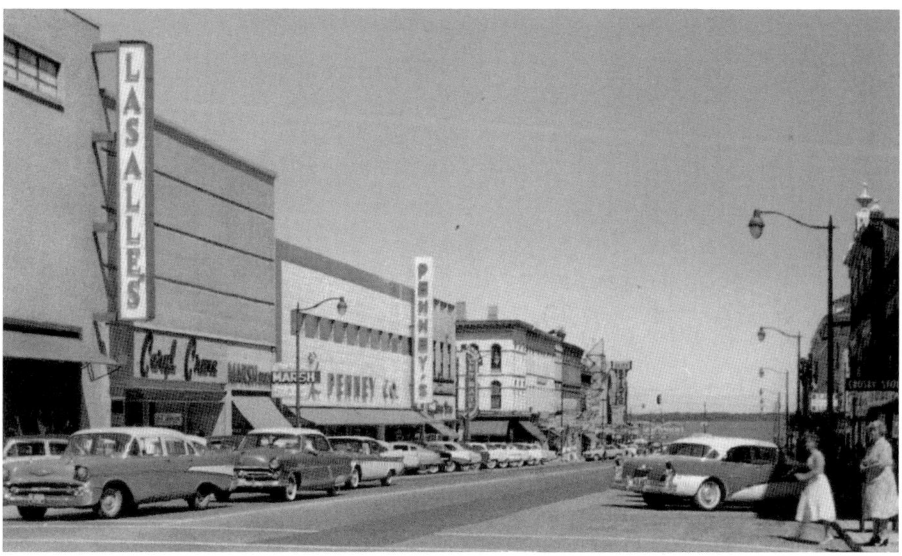


The LaSalle, Caryl Crane and J.C. Penney stores are seen on Columbus Avenue in this postcard photo, circa 1950s. *Sandusky Library Follett House Museum Archives.*

the LaSalle and J.C. Penney department stores. It sold shoes, sportswear and lingerie and had a bridal department and millinery. Women could buy everything from a Sunday hat to everyday shoes there.

Barb Vanasco, seventy-two, grew up in Sandusky and remembers shopping at Caryl Crane because it had higher-end clothes and a good selection.

"I still have my long leather coat from there," she said.

The store also had a location in Lorain, a city east of Sandusky, according to the 1954 business directory. By 1980, the Sandusky store had moved out of downtown to the Sandusky Mall.

"We worked hard at it for 30 years downtown, but merchandise was changing, and we always had to change with the times," B. Robert Shiff told the *Register* that year. "The downtown hours were not what the public was demanding, and parking was a problem."

The store closed in 1981.

## S.S. Kresge

S.S. Kresge was a popular chain store found in many towns, including Sandusky. Started in Detroit by Sebastian Spering Kresge, the chain was a five-and-dime store that sold everything a customer might need, from housewares to clothes, according to the Detroit Historical Society.

The Kresge stores ultimately became the K-Mart Corporation in the 1970s. In Sandusky, the Kresge store was located at 202 Columbus Avenue from the early 1920s to 1964, when it closed, the *Register* reported. For many years, there were two Kresge stores in the city, one at 202 Columbus Avenue and one at 236 Columbus Avenue, according to Sandusky business directories and a 1960 *Register* article. A picture the Sandusky Library has of one of the store's interiors shows a lunch counter, where shoppers could stop by for a snack or sandwich.

"The needs of the neighborhood around the store have changed to the point where a variety store no longer serves the community," Howard Vescelius, S.S. Kresge central region manager, told the *Register*.

A discount store called Jupiter opened in its place in 1965, the *Register* reported. The store was based on the sales model of K-Mart stores, Jupiter store manager Dan McCully told the *Register* in 1965.

Jupiter remained open until 1987. Today, the restaurant Small City Taphouse occupies the space.

## F.W. Woolworth

Another popular chain store that had a shop in downtown Sandusky was F.W. Woolworth. Like S.S. Kresge, it was a five-and-dime store with a lunch counter. The store opened around 1915 at 220 Columbus Avenue.

Vanasco and Jean Gardner, seventy-two, who also grew up in Sandusky, remember attending school at the nearby high school—which later became Adams Junior High—and walking to Woolworth's for lunch.

"We liked their french fries and their milkshakes," Gardner said. "It was a treat for me to go down there and eat."

Her family was friendly with the store manager, and his daughter was in Gardner and Vanasco's class in school. They liked to support the store and the family, Gardner said.

Woolworth's had everything from clothes to household necessities, Vanasco said. She remembers dyeing her hair there.

The pair also remember when fire gutted the store on January 5, 1960. The blaze started in the basement and ripped through the building, destroying it and the offices next to it, according to the *Register*. Later the same day, the fire broke out again, further devastating the structure, the newspaper reported the next day. Most of the store's contents were lost to the flames.

The building was so engulfed that a crowd stood outside and watched as all of the city's firefighters fought the blaze, the newspaper reported. Smoke caused the S.S. Kresge store at 202 Columbus Avenue to close for the day after the fire. Kresge's second store on Columbus Avenue, however, stayed open as usual.

Gardner's mother was a Red Cross volunteer, and Gardner remembers the agency setting up a relief area at one of the Kresge stores.

"For a long time after Woolworth's burned, you could still smell the smoke at Kresge's," Gardner said.

Like Kresge, Woolworth's had two stores in Sandusky at that time. The second was located in a shopping center outside of downtown, and Woolworth district superintendent Edward Dick told the *Register* that employees might be transferred there.

Firefighters determined the building's boiler was not to blame for the blaze, the *Register* reported on January 12, 1960. It is not known if a cause was ever identified.

Despite the destruction, F.W. Woolworth rebuilt the store and kept it open until December 1971.

A lack of business and competition from its second store at the Perkins Plaza shopping center prompted the company to close the downtown store, manager Ray Wolford told the *Register*.

"We're not doing the business we expected to do, and they think one store in Sandusky is plenty," Wolford told the newspaper.

Woolworth's later had a store at the Sandusky Mall.

## Strickfaden's Holiday Shop

Many locals remember Strickfaden's Holiday Shop and its German mechanical Santa as a Christmas tradition. The store grew to be a winter wonderland, the largest year-round Christmas shop in Ohio.

The store's roots start with J.C. Strickfaden, who opened a garage and service station in 1920 on South Columbus Avenue, according to the *Register*. In the late 1920s, Strickfaden opened a nursery business, the *Lorain Morning Journal* reported. It is not clear whether he opened the nursery in the same spot as the service station or elsewhere.

The company weathered the Great Depression, which started in 1929, and expanded into the landscaping business in 1933, according to the *Journal*. In 1937, the company started selling Christmas items, J.C. Strickfaden's son, Joe, told the newspaper.

"It was quite crude," he said. "We had fresh wreaths and door pieces, center pieces and a small beginning of ornaments."

World War II brought hardship. By then, the shop was located in the area where the NASA Plum Brook research station is today, just south of Sandusky.

The U.S. government told the Strickfadens and others in the area they had to move because the government planned to build the Plum Brook Ordnance Works there, according to the *Register*. The ordnance works made explosives for the war effort, and the factory displaced a good-sized community, said Ron Davidson, Sandusky Library special collections librarian.

"It was a shock," Joe recalled to the *Register* in 1993. "We didn't know where to go. Some that didn't have it so good were happy to get out and start over.

"Others, like us, were making a good living and didn't want to get out. We were the last ones to move."

After the war, J.C. Strickfaden bought forty acres of land on Bell Avenue and went back into business, according to the *Register*. An old barn, heated by a fireplace, served as the store. Business improved in the 1950s and '60s, and the store started selling lawn care products and home and yard furnishings. It also sold Christmas trees and had thousands shipped in by train, the *Register* reported.

The store kept expanding. In 1975, it became the largest year-round Christmas shop in Ohio, according to the *Register*. More than fifty trees with ornaments of different themes filled the store, and one room was devoted just to electrical and lighting needs.

The Strickfadens went to Europe and traveled across North America to find high-quality merchandise for their shop, including thousands of hand-painted, blown glass ornaments and handcrafted wooden nutcrackers and incense smokers from Germany, according to the *Register*. They offered personalized service to help customers find exactly what they wanted. One of the store's managers, Jean McDowell, told the *Journal* she remembered shipping a Christmas tree to Brazil one year.

"That's how we grew," Joe told the *Register*. "My father taught me you have to be willing to spend a buck to make a buck."

In 1981, the Strickfadens went to Germany and bought the mechanical Santa that many locals remember seeing in the store, according to the *Journal*. It cost $14,000.

Four generations of the family worked at the store. In 1993, Joe and his wife, Geraldine, decided to close the store and retire. He was seventy-nine, and she was eighty, according to the *Register*.

"It's hard to imagine a Christmas without strolling through Strickfaden's eye-dazzling Christmas displays, watching the large-scale model railroad with four separate trains winding through a village or talking to the life-like mechanical Santa," the *Register* reported.

Today, the lot where the business stood is a park, called Strickfaden Park. The mechanical Santa was put on display in 2009 for Christmastime at the Carousel Museum in Sandusky, according to the newspaper.

# 11
# SCHOOLS

As settlers came to Sandusky, their children needed to be educated. The first school in the city was a private school where Sallie Stimpson taught students whose parents paid tuition in 1818. The school was a log cabin on Wayne Street, according to the book *History of the Western Reserve Vol. 1* by Harriet Taylor Upton.

One-room schoolhouses popped up throughout Ohio, and by 1820, there were thirty-five of them in Erie County alone, the *Sandusky Register* reported. Eventually, Sanduskians elected officers to make decisions for the public school district and started consolidating those one-room schools into community schools.

Sandusky was one of the first school systems to introduce the graded system, meaning students were assessed and separated into grade levels, according to the *Register*. The district did this in 1848.

The city, a major stop on the Underground Railroad, also was ahead of the times with integration. Locals felt there needed to be educational opportunities for African American students and opened a school for them. In 1853, the school had twenty to thirty students, according to *Sandusky Area Sesquicentennial* book published in 1968.

Then in 1861, Sandusky Schools' first superintendent, M.F. Cowdery, ordered the students to be integrated into the public school system, according to the book.

Many of the schools built in the 1800s still stand in Sandusky. Some are still used as schools, and others have different purposes.

When most of Sandusky's schools were built, they were made to be neighborhood schools and catered to families living around them, said Bill Biehl of Sandusky, former principal at the now closed Madison School.

Like many buildings in Sandusky, most of the schools were constructed of limestone, a material readily available because of the area's geology. Most of the schools were named for the streets on which they were located. Additions were added to many of them over the years.

"They were well built and well maintained," said Biehl, who was principal at Madison for twenty-one years. "The state or anyone who came in would comment on how well things were maintained."

The school district closely watched the buildings' condition and made a list of projects that needed to be done. It then raised money through ballot issues or saved money to complete the work, Biehl said.

"Taxpayers have been very supportive of the schools," he said.

## Old Courthouse

In 1828, residents decided to build an academy on the public square, on what is today Columbus Avenue. One room was finished in 1834, and it was used for an academy taught by Miss Mills—her first name is lost to history—and by the Congregational church, according to Upton's book.

Sandusky was named the Erie County seat in 1838, but it didn't have a courthouse. So the academy building, which was not yet finished, was turned into a courthouse, according to the *Register*.

The building was used as a courthouse until 1874, when the current courthouse was built across Columbus Avenue from the academy building. The building was used again as a school until it was torn down in 1886, wrote Follett House Museum historians Virginia Steinemann and Helen Hansen in the "Follett House Scrapbook," a regular historical feature the pair wrote for the *Register*.

## Adams Junior High

An imposing limestone building between Adams and Washington Streets, Adams Junior High was built as a high school next to the old courthouse/academy building, according to the *Register*. It was built in 1867.

Adams replaced the city's first high school, which burned down in the late 1860s on the same site, according to Sandusky Library Archives. Sandusky was one of the first cities in Ohio to have a high school, according to the "Follett House Scrapbook."

Biehl's mother attended Adams when it was still a high school. The steps of the building are worn from thousands of students going up and down them over the years, he said.

For many years, Adams Junior High housed just seventh grade, but when Jackson Junior High closed in 2009, eighth graders moved there as well, said Bill Ehrnsberger, school district brand development and retention and recruitment coordinator. In 2012, the district moved the seventh and eighth grades to the Sandusky High School, he said.

The district still uses the building and runs an online learning program for students who don't fit a traditional high school atmosphere, Ehrnsberger said. They earn a regular diploma, just in a setting more specialized to their needs.

Part of the building is leased to North Point Educational Service Center, an agency that offers support—like special education and early childhood programs—for school districts in the Sandusky region. Adams is the second-oldest school building still in active use in Ohio, according to the school district.

## East and West Market Schools

Two of the first schools in the city were the East Market School, 328 East Market Street, and West Market School, 207 Fulton Street. They were built in 1845 in two of the bigger areas of commerce in the city, and they are nearly identical limestone buildings. A third school was built at the same time on Madison Street, but it no longer stands, the *Register* reported in 1964.

The East Market School was also called the East Market Primary and Secondary School and was used as a school building into the 1870s, according to the "Follett House Scrapbook." In the 1880s, Fred J. Hinckey used the building for his blacksmith and power forging business, where he made ice tools and stonecutters. He built an addition to the building.

After the blacksmith business closed, the addition had various uses over the years, including as a storage area, a laundry, a Chinese restaurant and a meeting place for church groups, according to the "Follett House Scrapbook." The school building and two commercial buildings on the site

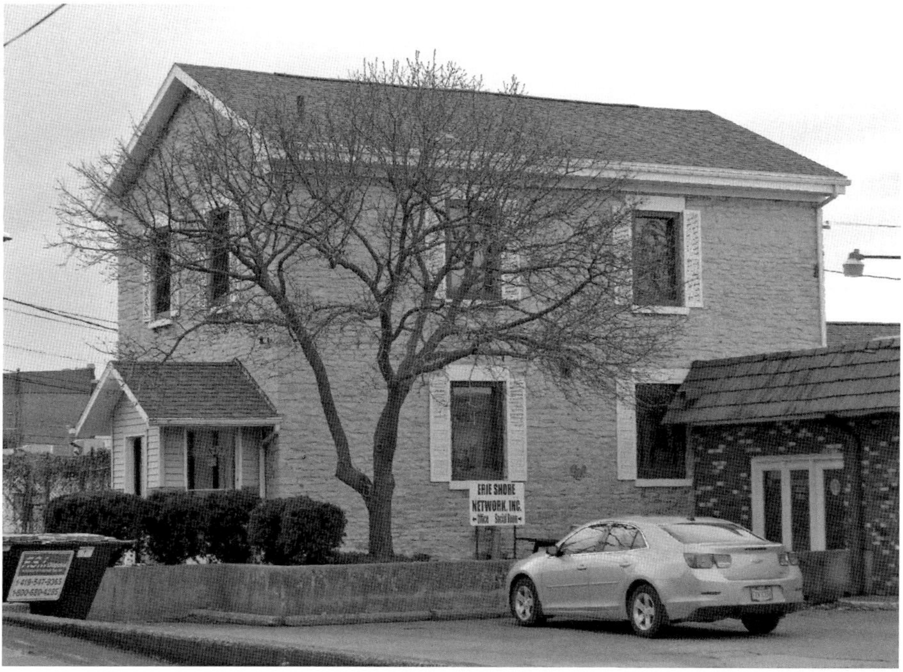


*Above*: The East Market School still stands and was incorporated into a drive-through business. *Photo by Kristina Smith.*

*Right*: The West Market School, the brother of the East Market School, was one of Sandusky's first city schools. *Sandusky Library Follett House Museum Archives.*

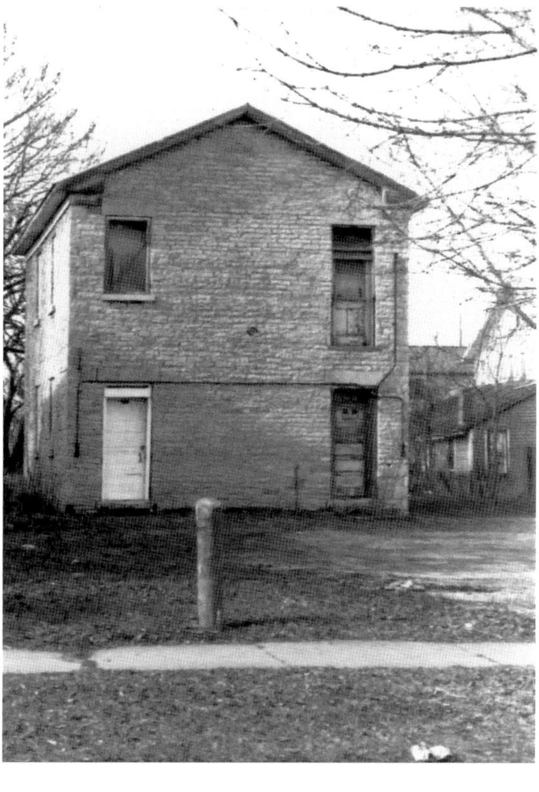

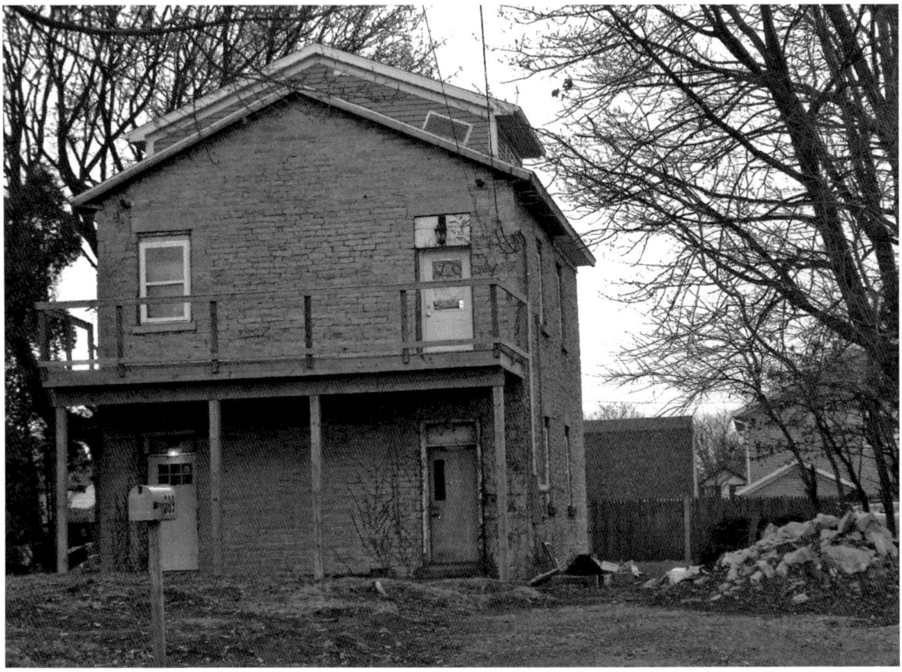

The West Market School building was renovated into living space. *Photo by Kristina Smith.*

were combined. In 1989, Louis Schultz Jr. repaired and restored the school building, according to the "Follett House Scrapbook."

Today, the buildings are part of a drive-through convenience store. The stone school building still stands, easily recognizable in the small complex.

After the West Market School's days as a house of education ended, a manufacturing company was housed there in the early 1900s, according to the "Follett House Scrapbook." It then sat vacant for many years. By 1964, the building was used to store lumber, the *Register* reported. By 2010, a young entrepreneur had bought the building and made plans to turn it into a home, according to the *Register*.

## Madison School

The first Madison School was built in 1872. It stood until 1939, when one of President Franklin Delano Roosevelt's Great Depression–era projects employed workers to build a new school in its place, Biehl said.

The second Madison School was built of red brick with a slate roof. The new school was built in an L shape around the old building, Ehrnsberger said. When construction was finished, students helped carry desks and chairs from the old building into the new, and the old building was torn down, he said.

Biehl, a Sandusky native, grew up in the neighborhood and attended kindergarten there.

"It used to be a neighborhood school when there were more kids in the neighborhood," he said. "I don't believe they even had a lunch program until probably the 1970s. Everyone went home for lunch."

Biehl returned to the school in 1973 as a student teacher and then again as a teacher in the 1980s. At that time, the school district clustered grade levels, and the third and fourth grades were located at Madison.

The school served grades kindergarten through four at the time it closed at the end of the 2008–09 school year, Biehl said. The district closed it because of declining enrollment and for financial reasons, he said.

The district sold Madison School and two other closed schools, Barker and Campbell, for five dollars to Richard Koonce, Biehl said. The district sold the buildings at such a low price because they would be too expensive to maintain, especially if they were not in use, Biehl said.

Koonce then gave the buildings to his church, Spirit and Truth Ministries of Sandusky, according to Erie County Auditor's Office records. The church still uses the Madison building.

## Barker School

One of the district's limestone buildings, Barker School was built in 1874. It also served as a neighborhood school.

In its last years, the school served as an alternative setting for students with emotional problems and other issues. Teachers and staff there worked with them to help them meet their potential, Toni DeLuca, a counselor at the school, told the *Port Clinton News Herald* during a June 2006 interview.

"A lot of them don't like school because they've never had any success," DeLuca told the newspaper. "We try to find a way they can be successful. To show them that they can do it and they are smart enough is so rewarding."

Students, staff and alumni had a picnic before school let out that summer and shared memories of their days at the historic building. The following fall, the students at Barker were moved to Sandusky High School.

"It's sad," DeLuca told the *News Herald*. "It's got a lot of memories of all the students who've been here over the years."

After Koonce gave the school to Spirit and Truth Ministries, the church sold it to a private resident for $35,000, according to Erie County Auditor's Office records. A daycare opened in the building, which is on the National Register of Historic Places.

## Sycamore School

Sycamore School was built in 1876. Ray Niehm, a Sandusky native who lives just outside the city in Perkins Township, remembers growing up in the neighborhood and attending Sycamore School.

He remembers that the recess area had one area for boys and another for girls. He and his classmates went home for lunch every day.

Years later, he returned to Sycamore as building principal. He was also Monroe School's principal, and he split time between the two. He would drop his children off for class at Monroe, spend the morning at Sycamore, pick the kids up and go home for lunch and then spend the afternoon at Monroe.

"Everyone went home for lunch," Niehm said. "We had no cafeterias back then."

By 1977, the school's enrollment was declining, and its future was uncertain, the *Register* reported.

It stayed open until around 1980 or 1982, Ehrnsberger said. Then the three-story limestone structure was sold in 1984 and turned into an apartment building, according to the "Follett House Scrapbook." The building is on the National Register of Historic Places.

## Campbell School

Campbell School was built in 1884, and it was used as a school until the early 2000s. It had a clock tower, but a tornado destroyed that feature in the 1920s, Bill Ehrnsberger said.

Ehrnsberger, a Sandusky native, and his mother both attended kindergarten there, and he remembers it as a massive building. The last addition, built in 1991, brought it to 28,860 square feet, according to the school district.

"It's a really neat building," he said.

Campbell School is on the National Register of Historic Places.

Koonce bought Campbell, Barker and Madison schools because he was looking for a place to open a center for youth that would offer tutoring, mentoring and recreational opportunities, he said when he spoke to Ebenezer Church of God in Christ in Fremont in February 2010.

The idea for a youth center came to him after a drunken driver smashed into the back of his car in 2005 on the Ohio Turnpike, the *News-Messenger* reported.

As Koonce drifted in and out of consciousness, he felt God was telling him, "I've got work for you to do," the newspaper quoted him as saying.

Koonce believed that work was to help local youth, especially African American children, realize their importance and reach their goals. A youth center would be a good way to accomplish that, he decided. So he worked with the pastor at his church and other church officials in Sandusky on the project.

They opened Nehemiah Partners of Sandusky in the Campbell building. The program offers educational and faith services, mentoring and activities.

## Monroe School

Built in 1894, Monroe School was another stately building. In the old days, the building was heated by burning coal in the basement, Niehm said. When gas heat was installed, the school converted the coal room into a kindergarten classroom. It had all new furniture and was painted to cover any trace of its former use.

"It was beautiful," he said. "It was the prettiest room around at that time in Sandusky schools. It was very unusual, but very nice."

Niehm remembers taking the district's superintendent to see it.

"He said: 'Wow, it's really something,'" Niehm said.

Niehm, who retired in 1987, has fond memories of the schools, including going out for recess with the students and playing baseball with them. In 1970, Venice Heights Elementary School opened, and he became principal there.

"I loved it very much," he said of his time in the school district. "I enjoyed the children. I enjoyed the parents."

Monroe School closed in 2006, Ehrnsberger said. A church bought the building and used it for a while, Biehl said. It is not clear whether the building is still in use.

The building is on the National Register of Historic Places.

## Jackson Junior High School

Jackson Junior High is one of the more unusual buildings in the district. The mostly redbrick building is really three buildings linked together and measures a massive 86,994 square feet.

The original structure was built in 1898 to be a community center, said Ehrnsberger, who attended Jackson and other district schools as well. It housed car shows and boat shows, and it was designed so the doors could be removed and vehicles could be driven up a ramp inside, he said. His grandmother won an archery competition held there.

The building also has an organ and a swimming pool, which is located below the gym, as well as a sound system, which was the latest technology when it was installed, he said.

Through the years, a limestone building on the property that was once a Lutheran school and another building were incorporated into the structure, he said.

"It was extremely disjointed in how it was built," he said.

Jackson housed eighth graders until 2009, when they moved to Adams Junior High. In 2012, the junior high was moved to the high school.

The school district still uses Jackson's pool and gym and houses a learning program there. The building is on the National Register of Historic Places.

## Follett House

Locals know the Follett House at 404 Wayne Street as a museum and keeper of local history, but it once was a school. The house was the home of Oran Follett, who was one of the first school directors for Sandusky public schools, the *Register* reported in 1947. The school directors were the forerunners of the school board.

Follett's house was built from 1834 to 1837, according to Sandusky Library archives. The school system started using it in 1939, said Ron Davidson, Sandusky Library special collections librarian.

The district had a large home economics program where Sandusky High School students could practice cooking, cleaning, doing laundry and sewing in a domestic setting, according to the *Register*. Sandusky schools also ran a school of practical nursing there for students, ages seventeen to fifty-five, Davidson said.

At some point, both of those programs ended. The Follett House officially became a museum on July 4, 1976, and was run by the Sandusky Library, Davidson said. The school district didn't deed the house to the library until 1982, he said.

## Buckeye Business College

Buckeye Business College—later known as Buckeye and Great Western Business College and then Sandusky Business College—opened in 1866 on Columbus Avenue, according to records on file at the Rutherford B. Hayes Presidential Center.

It was advertised as a college for commercial and business education of young men and boys. Boys ages fourteen and older and men of all ages were accepted, according to a flier for the college.

"Many young men have now a fine business position, who without this course of practical training, would have been drones in business and society all their lives," a promotional paper for the college said. "The course is short and comprehensive and prepares the pupil directly for active life."

Classes included bookkeeping, penmanship and German. There was a business department class where a student received cash to use as capital, a journal and a ledger that he used to buy and sell merchandise while balancing his budget, according to fliers for the school.

At some point, women were admitted to the school, according to the sesquicentennial book. Tuition in the 1870s was forty-five dollars for men and forty dollars for women. The school closed in the mid-1940s.

# 12
# LOST TOURIST ATTRACTIONS

From roadside oddities to natural wonders, the Sandusky area has been home to some popular tourist attractions that have closed and faded into history.

The area's geology helped make for some mysterious and popular stops, including a seemingly bottomless hole of clear blue water and caves with what appeared to be underground rivers. Other stops were man-made works, including a ship with a gruesome legend that entertained crowds of all ages.

For different reasons, ranging from declining attendance to disaster, they eventually closed or were destroyed. Those who were fortunate enough to see them when they were open have fond memories of these unusual attractions.

## "Convict Ship" *Success*

Thousands of people watched from the shoreline as flames burst from a 106-year-old ship in Lake Erie off Port Clinton on July 4, 1946.

So many people stopped on Perry Street to gawk at the spectacular blaze that police were called in to keep traffic moving, the *Port Clinton Herald and Republican* reported on July 12, 1946. The boat had been beached off Perry Street—in about fourteen feet of water near the area where Perry Street turns into East Harbor Road at the city limits—since August, when its owner tried to bring it from its last home in Sandusky to Port Clinton.

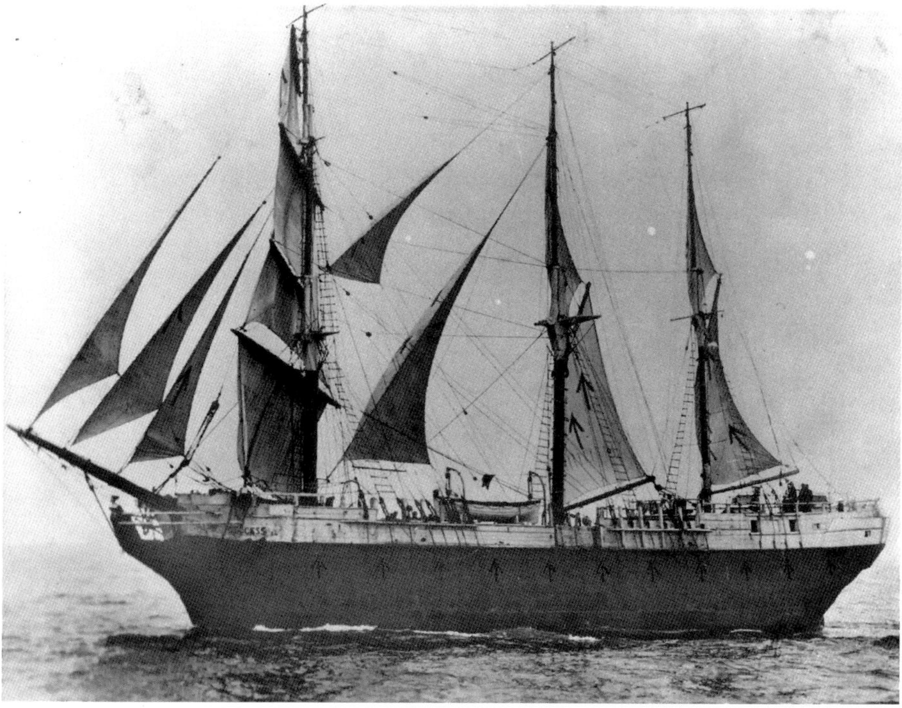

The *Success* was a ship whose legend was largely based on false stories. Made of teak, it was an interesting craft without its embellished history. *Rutherford B. Hayes Presidential Center/ Charles Frohman Collection.*

"In a blaze of flame, she passed out of existence on a very appropriate day—the Fourth of July," the newspaper reported.

At about 4:00 p.m., the ship caught fire, and the flames ravaged it to the waterline by midnight. The blaze, believed to be arson, was a sad ending to the *Success*, a storied and unusual ship. Throughout its career, the *Success* had been an ornate trading ship, a floating prison in Australia and then a rather gruesome tourist attraction that traveled the world, according to newspaper accounts. Myriad famous people visited the ship, from composer John Philip Sousa to Harry Houdini, who staged an escape from the vessel in 1913, said Rich Norgard of Catawba Island, who has spent decades researching the ship's history.

At the time it burned, the *Success* also was reputed to be the oldest ship in the world and a prison that ferried prisoners from England to Australia while the jail keepers committed horrific acts of torture and punishment against the prisoners. Those claims, however, weren't true, according to Rutherford

B. Hayes Presidential Center's collection of records regarding the ship. They were yarns spun to add to the ship's notoriety and sell tickets for people to see its house-of-horrors cells and "history."

The *Success* was interesting enough in its own right. It was built in 1840 in Burma as a trading ship. It was made of teak, an exceptionally sturdy type of wood that was rare and expensive by the 1940s, and measured 135 feet long and had a 30-foot beam, according to the *Herald and Republican*. Historical records give different amounts for its tonnage, but it is accurate to say that the ship was big and heavy.

"It was just a really unique example of shipbuilding from that period from that place," Norgard said. "There really isn't anything else left like it."

After the *Success*'s trading days, the ship took settlers to Australia. In 1852, the crew abandoned the boat in Australia in favor of joining the gold rush in that country, according to the Hayes Center.

*Success* didn't stay empty for long, though. The Victorian government was running out of room to house people charged with crimes and bought the *Success* and four other large ships to be floating prisons. The ship was moored off Williamstown and first housed male prisoners. Then it was a detention center for women and boys.

In 1885, the government decided its "felon fleet" was inhumane and got rid of the ships, according to the Hayes Center. An entrepreneur bought the boat and tried to turn it into a museum that showed the horrors of Australian prison life, but the venture was not successful, according to the Hayes Center. Ten years later, a syndicate tried its luck with the concept and fared much better.

During those years, Joseph Harvie managed the boat and turned it into a popular attraction that traveled Europe. Although the ship had wax figures portrayed in various states of prison life, the embellishment of the ship's history didn't start until later, Norgard said.

Harvie's daughter, Hilda, recalled stories of running around the deck and seeing the wax figures in various states of frightful treatment, Hilda's granddaughter, Australian native Melissa Ackart, told the *Port Clinton News Herald* in 1997.

After its success in Europe, the ship changed hands again in 1911. American David Smith bought it and decided to send it on a North American tour, Norgard said.

Smith was a showman who knew how to draw crowds, and it was under his tenure that the ship's history became twisted and falsified—with excellent results. Tourists lined up to see the various punishments and torture, from prisoners being flogged with a whip called the "cat o' nine tails" and dipped in salt water afterward to sitting in solitary in one of the dungeon-like cells on the ship's lower decks below the waterline.

These ghoulish exhibits of how prisoners were treated also were exaggerated, according to the Hayes Center. And it was under Smith's leadership that the false claim that the *Success* took convicts from England to Australia started, Norgard said.

Advertising pamphlets from the 1920s–'40s said it was built in 1790, but that wasn't true either. Historians believe someone guessed at how old the ship was and settled on that year. Then promoting took over, making it seem like fact, Norgard said.

"It was published and republished by press agents and so forth that it became its de facto history," Norgard said. "The Australians, for years, had been publishing the real history of it, but it never got through to the American press. It's a testament to [Smith] as a promoter."

The notoriety of the "convict ship" was a huge draw. More than 21 million people visited the *Success*, according to advertising pamphlets.

According to a 1924 pamphlet,

> *The only remaining link between the old and the new, the convict ship now serves a purpose of good where it long signified oppression. In remembering man of what he once countenanced and once suffered in the name of law and justice, it now serves the noble purpose of arousing public conscience to the realization that even in this twentieth century, the forms of justice and the conduct of prisons may be improved.*
>
> *It brought home the lesson to other countries and it is now pointing out the lesson in these Great United States, whose correctional institutions lead the world.*

The Australians, however, deeply resented the claims the ship's promoters and crew made regarding prisoner treatment, according to the Hayes Center.

The myths wouldn't draw people forever. The Great Depression and World War II took their toll. Smith wisely sold the boat by the end of the 1920s.

"Smith had made a lot of money on the thing," Norgard said. "Pretty much the heyday of the ship was the mid- to late '20s. It did very, very well. It probably made him a millionaire."

The next owner was Frank Jontzen, who owned a Cleveland printing business. He brought the boat back to the Great Lakes, where it continued to tour. The ship visited Sandusky in September 1938 and was open for tours at the foot of Jackson Street for a "nominal charge," the *Sandusky Star-Journal* reported on September 22, 1938. The boat stayed for about two weeks.

*Success* then docked in Cleveland and stayed there until 1942, Norgard said. Cleveland would be the last port where it was a tourist attraction.

"Jontzen was not nearly the promoter Smith was," he said. "Its drawing power had been greatly diminished."

The government needed the dock space for the war effort, so the *Success* had to go, Norgard said. Harry Van Stack, a South African native who had given lectures aboard the boat for years about cannibalism, black magic and other topics, found a spot for it in Sandusky. By this time, the boat was in pretty bad shape and no longer seaworthy.

In Sandusky, a bad storm sunk the *Success* at its dock in the area of what is today Deepwater Marina, according to the Sandusky Maritime Museum. Van Stack salvaged some of its artifacts, including beautifully carved teak ornaments, shackles, the cat o' nine tails and a few other items from the prison museum portion of the ship. His widow later donated them to the Hayes Center, which loaned them to the maritime museum, where they are on display.

Walter Kolbe was the *Success*'s final owner. He towed it to Port Clinton in 1945, but the ship was too big to make it into the Portage River. It ran aground to its final resting place as Kolbe was trying to tow it to waterfront property he owned, Norgard said. Kolbe had begun stripping it of valuables before it burned, according to the Hayes Center.

Despite its end, the *Success* remains a special ship. Ernie Washington of Catawba Island, a seasoned diver who has explored shipwrecks in Lake Erie and other lakes, found the ship decades ago and recovered a variety of artifacts from it, including two cleats, a safe, doors and even pieces of the figures used in the torture recreations. He did this before maritime law was enacted prohibiting the taking of items from shipwrecks.

During one of his many dives on the wreckage, Washington came across a wooden foot and shoe of one of the dummies.

"I thought this was somebody's bone and leg," he said. "I about had a fit. I threw it down."

It didn't take him long to realize what it was. The foot and shoe are now on display at his home. The cleats can be seen in front of Wendy's and at New Wave Dive Shop, both in Port Clinton.

Washington took Ackart to the site and dived on it with her in 1997 so she could see the place her grandmother loved so much in her childhood.

Today, a few divers still ask New Wave staff about the *Success* so that they, too, can see what attracted so many people to this unusual ship, owner Rod Althaus said.

"It's one of the most interesting ships ever just because it's been in so many places and done so many things," Norgard said. "People were married on it. People died on it."

## Blue Hole: "Ohio's Greatest Natural Wonder"

Just outside Sandusky is the small town of Castalia, named after the Kastalia spring in Delphi, Greece. The town got the moniker because of its natural springs, which fed underground streams and phenomena known as blue holes.

Blue holes are actually springs where groundwater and surface water that drained into sinkholes comes up through the ground, said Douglas Aden, mapping geologist for the Ohio Department of Natural Resources, Division of Geological Survey.

The rock in the Castalia area is a porous carbonate rock, known as limestone, which can filter water and be dissolved by water. Rain, which becomes slightly acidic as it picks up carbon dioxide in the atmosphere, flows through cracks in the rock.

Over time, those cracks widen, creating caves and sinkholes. In northwest Ohio, the material on top of the rock is glacial till, including sediments, clay, silt, sand and gravel.

At the same time, water filters through the rock and flows underground, making passages filled with water, sometimes referred to as underground rivers. Aden said the term "underground river" is also a misnomer; it's a network of cracks where water percolates through.

A blue hole forms through erosion from water. The term "blue hole" also is a misnomer because they aren't actually blue, Aden said.

"It's kind of an optical illusion," said Aden, who specializes in the geology that creates blue holes. "The water is very clear, so it reflects the sky. If you had a glass of it, it would not be blue."

There are several blue holes around Castalia, but one was a bona fide tourist attraction that brought thousands of people to the area for decades. Pictures through the years show the same thing: people standing along the banks and gazing into the seemingly bottomless and impossibly blue water. And fashions show that it enthralled people over generations, from women in their Sunday best dresses and big hats in the 1920s and '30s to the shorts and T-shirts of the '80s.

Early commercial development can be thanked for the Blue Hole's existence. The Blue Hole is connected to Cold Creek in Castalia, a prime trout stream fed by the springs that maintain a constant temperature of forty-eight to fifty degrees.

In 1810, pioneer Dorcartus Snow decided to take advantage of the pristine creek and built a gristmill there. The dam he built to support the mill changed water levels. That caused pressure on the rock in the area of the Blue Hole, causing it to collapse and form a sinkhole that would become the tourist attraction, according to the *Register*.

Over the years, the Blue Hole would continue to collapse and get bigger until it was seventy-five feet in diameter in 1914, the year the *Register* reported locals were concerned because the Blue Hole's clear water was churning and roiled.

When settlers arrived in the Castalia area, the area springs were mainly used as a medicine camp for American Indians in the area, according to the book *Castalia, Cold Creek, and the Blue Hole* by Glenn C. Kuebeler.

"Indians attributed great curative powers to the clear, cold water," according to the *Register*.

To the American Indians and early European settlers, Cold Creek was a novelty and a mystery. They were puzzled because the stream maintained a constant temperature even in cold snaps and heat waves, but fish could not survive there.

Settlers felt that the clear creek, which Adan said is cold because the water has been underground for so long, seemed like ideal habitat for trout. But unsettlingly, fish stocked there rose to the surface in a dead mass.

"The stream and surrounding area gained a reputation for being ominous, mysterious and perhaps haunted," according to a 1973 informational pamphlet Owens-Illinois, former owner of one of the trout clubs in the area, wrote about the area.

So early settlers kept using the stream as a power source for mills until locals realized in the late 1800s that the stream didn't circulate enough to have adequate oxygen levels, according to the pamphlet.

The water was low in oxygen because it was underground and not exposed to elements that would mix the layers and add oxygen, Adan said. Once dams and spillways were added, the water turned over, providing oxygen to support trout, and the stream became the fishery it is today. Aerators are now used to keep the water flowing and oxygenated, Adan said. Like Cold Creek, the Blue Hole had no oxygen and kept a constant cold temperature.

All of this added to the Blue Hole's legend and lure. The cone-shaped pond was believed to be bottomless. One oft-told story was that a horse and carriage disappeared into the hole one night and never resurfaced.

"Those are old wives' tales," said Steve Sessler, manager of the Castalia Trout Club, which owns the Blue Hole.

The hole has a bottom, he said, estimating that it is about forty feet from the surface.

Nonetheless, the public found the natural phenomenon fascinating. In 1925, Leonard Hacker and Claire Goodwin leased the land around the hole from property owner Castalia Trout Club and opened it to the public, according to Kuebeler's book. They put a fence around the hole and added walkways, footbridges, a picnic area and a concession stand. At that time, admission to "Ohio's Greatest Natural Wonder" was ten cents.

During its peak from the '20s to '40s, 165,000 people visited the Blue Hole a year, *Cleveland Scene* magazine reported in 1999.

"I can remember traffic being backed up several miles coming into Castalia," said Kuebeler, who did maintenance work at the Blue Hole when he was a teen in the '50s. "For big weekends, thousands of people were coming in.

"At the time, it was a neat place to go to see the trout. They'd buy popcorn and throw it to the fish. The fish would jump out and catch the popcorn."

Sessler worked a maintenance job at the Blue Hole when he was in high school in the 1980s. He remembers visitors throwing coins into the hole to watch if they reached the bottom.

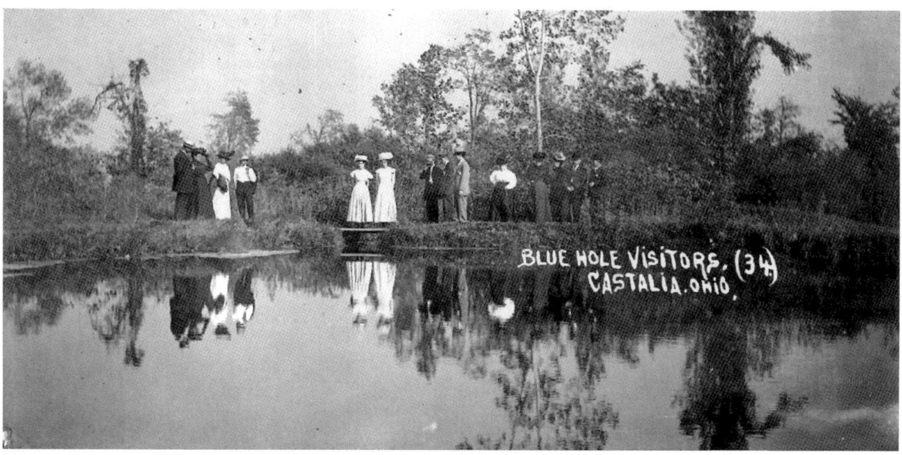


The Blue Hole drew visitors for more than a century. *Rutherford B. Hayes Presidential Center/ Charles Frohman Collection.*

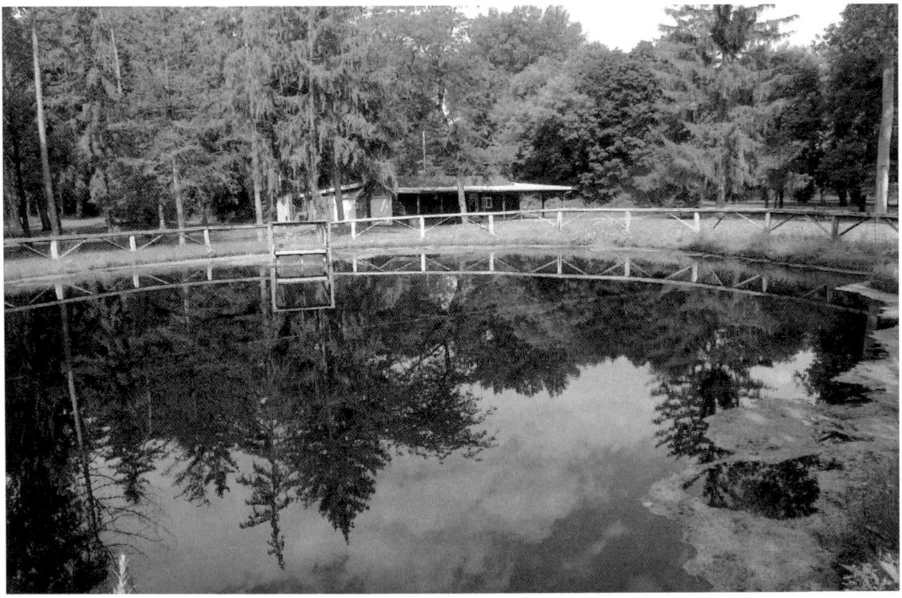

The Blue Hole is closed to the public but remains a natural wonder. *Photo by Jonathon Bird.*

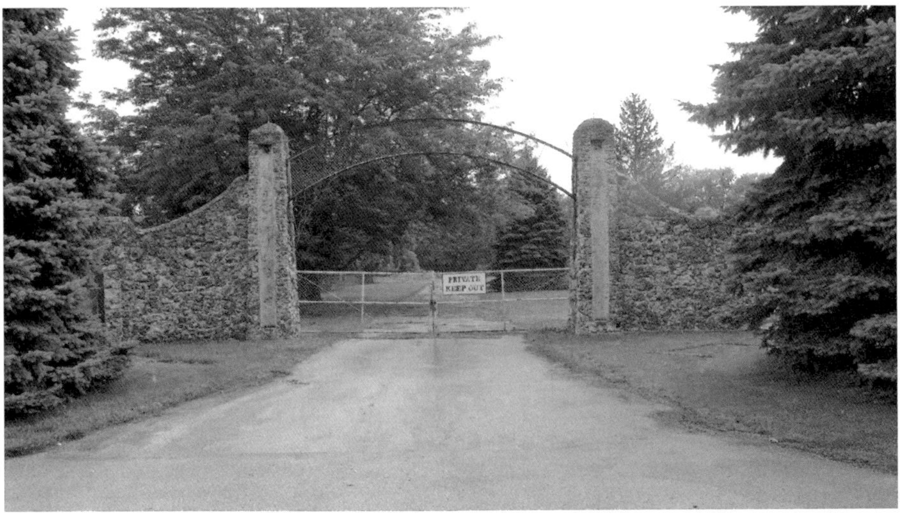


The Blue Hole's gate is still visible to passersby, but they cannot enter. *Photo by Jonathon Bird.*

The Blue Hole's popularity began to wane, and upkeep costs continued to rise, Sessler said. By the time it closed in 1990, twenty-five thousand people had visited the park that year.

Today, the large stone gate that once was the entrance to the Blue Hole still stands. Instead of the letters advertising the Blue Hole, there is a sign that reads "Private Keep Out."

The wood and chain fence that surrounded the Blue Hole and walkways are still there, although some weeds have grown up around them. The concession stand is now a workshop for the trout club, and the bathrooms have been torn down.

Yet the Blue Hole's lure remains, Sessler said.

"People ask about it all the time," he said. "We'll get calls of people wanting to see it, saying, 'I was there when I was a kid.'"

Sessler sends those who drive to the private trout club with the hope of seeing the Blue Hole to the nearby Castalia State Fish Hatchery run by the Ohio Department of Natural Resources. Another blue hole—which is often confused with the former tourist attraction—is located there and is open to the public.

## Crystal Rock Cave

Not far from the Blue Hole is Crystal Rock Cave, another bygone tourist attraction created by the area's geology. The cave, located in the Crystal Rock development on the Sandusky Bay, is connected to Brewery Cave, and the water flowing through Brewery Cave was used in brewing the Kuebeler-Stang Brewery's Crystal Rock Beer.

Locals knew about the caves as early as 1893. That year, the Mustcash Company made a deal with the City of Sandusky to pipe water from the caves to town. But the agreement ultimately fell through, said Jim Norrocky, Crystal Rock Cave's current owner. Instead, the company sold Crystal Rock Springs water in bottles and to the brewery.

In the 1900s, the caves became a tourist attraction. A dance hall was built in the area around 1904, according to the *Register*. The hall was popular in the '20s, and Guy Lombardo performed there, Norrocky said.

"It started out as kind of a high-class dance hall," he said.

In the late '30s, the dance hall was converted into a skating rink, according to the *Register*. The building burned down in January 1964.

During the '20s, the caves were accessible, but no one had carved out a good entrance with proper headroom for visitors. That changed in 1930 when Fred Hess found the hole that led to the caves and crawled inside. He

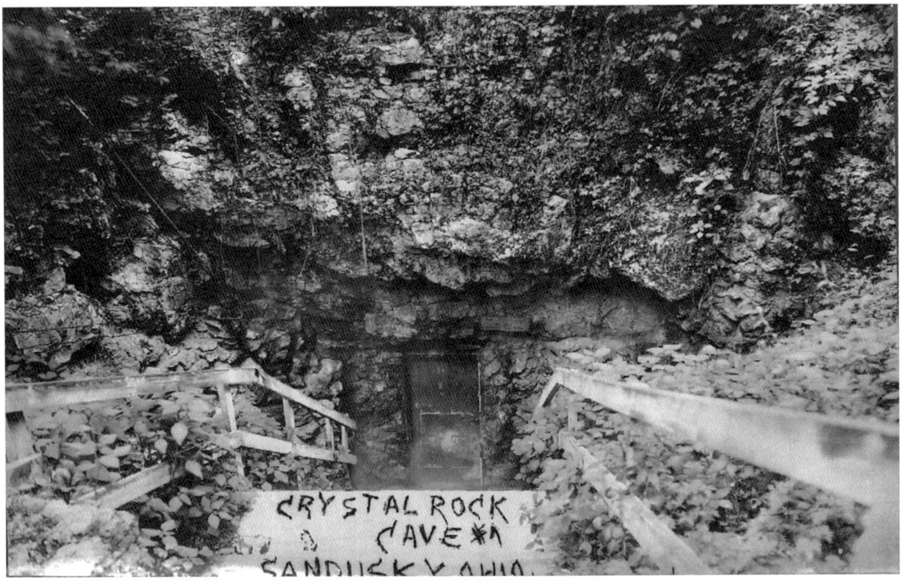


This is the entrance to Crystal Rock Cave in the days it was open to the public. *Rutherford B. Hayes Presidential Center/Charles Frohman Collection.*

thought the formations of stalactites on the ceiling and stalagmites coming up from the floor combined with what he called an underground river at the bottom would make the cave a roadside tourist attraction, the *Register* reported in 1933. Hess dug an entrance and flight of steps into Crystal Rock Cave and started offering tours.

"The caves have been open to the public for the past three years, and some days, as many as 500 visitors stop to enjoy the strangely beautiful mysterious sight that meets the eye 50 feet below the earth's surface," the newspaper reported. "Thousands visiting the park go through the cave, marveling at the sight of the silent river in its depths, so clear that a depth of many feet seems only a few inches."

The *Register* called the caves two of the most interesting caverns in Ohio.

"Mystery abounds in this underground body of water coming to be known as 'Ohio's Lost River,'" the newspaper reported.

Norrocky remembers the caves being open for tours while he was growing up in the 1950s. They were closed in the '60s.

Norrocky helped Ted Winkel clean up the caves and reopen them to the public in the 1970s. Winkel also added a campground, nature trails and picnic areas.

Brochures for the attraction at that time touted Crystal Rock Cave's unusual formations, including "the Alligator," "Large Set of Teeth" and "Elephant Head." The materials advertised the area as Crystal Caves Park and touted it as a family fun area that included a theater.

The park, however, closed within a decade, Norrocky said. As Cedar Point continued to grow and gain more visitors, the caves—and other small attractions like the Blue Hole—struggled, he said.

Norrocky bought ten acres that include Crystal Rock Cave a few years ago. He sealed off the cave entrance to keep people from wandering in and possibly falling and getting hurt. On the neighboring property, a home was built above Brewery Cave.

"I don't think the caves at Crystal Rock will ever be open to the public again," he said. "I have no intention of opening my cave to the public again."

The campground, called Crystal Rock Campground, remains open.

## Johnson's Island Pleasure Resort

On July 3, 1894, a resort that would give Cedar Point some serious, albeit short-lived, competition opened on nearby Johnson's Island on the Sandusky Bay.

Best known as the site of a prison for Confederate prisoners of war during the Civil War, the small island also was a picturesque spot to vacation. It started with a main pavilion and other structures that were covered in canvas because the owners wanted to get something together quickly to compete with Cedar Point, according to the Johnson's Island Preservation Society, which runs a small museum at the Ohio Veterans Home in Sandusky. Cedar Point is just across the bay from the island, and its rides are clearly visible from the island's shore.

The structures would later be replaced with a wooden pavilion that included a dance floor and guestrooms. A restaurant also was built there, and electricity was installed by 1896.

The resort did well, providing guests with cool, shaded spots to relax in the setting of former forts related to the prisoner depot and Union officers' quarters. It also offered music and dancing several nights a week, orchestra performances on Sundays and unusual entertainers that included contortionists.

The resort accommodated large groups seeking conventions and retreats, which added another facet to its appeal. By 1897, it was drawing crowds of three thousand to five thousand people, according to the preservation society's website.

The success didn't last long. On August 8, 1897, a trapeze artist's performance turned deadly.

She was suspended on a trapeze between two hot-air balloons when one of the balloons failed to ascend. A man fired a gun, which contained live rounds, as a signal to her to release her parachute. Instead of shooting the gun into the air, the man fired into the crowd. The bullet hit and killed a man, whose widow sued the resort for $10,000, according to the preservation society.

The incident and a fire at the main pavilion four months later were disastrous for the resort and forced it to close.

"Residents of Sandusky had to helplessly watch the building burn because they had no way to reach the island due to the early winter ice on Sandusky Bay," according to the society's website.

But that would not be the end of the resort. Steamboat captains Charles Goodside and Andrew Geisendorfer of Sandusky reopened the resort in 1904, according to the society. Goodside was a former Cedar Point employee, according to *Cedar Point: Queen of American Watering Places* by David W. Francis and Diane DeMali Francis. Goodside and Geisendorfer built a new pavilion and added a midway with a Ferris wheel, shooting gallery and carousel. The resort also offered baseball games, boat rentals, roller skating and vaudeville shows.

Although the island resort seemed to be thriving, Cedar Point had been taken over by George A. Boeckling, who returned it to its glory and made competing with it harder for the Johnson's Island resort. In 1908, Cedar Point bought the Johnson's Island Pleasure Resort Company and eliminated it as a competitor for good.

## Prehistoric Forest

Prehistoric Forest was a roadside attraction that generations of families visited over the years. The park was a wooded area where visitors could walk among life-sized replicas of dinosaurs and visit Mystery Hill, a cabin that defied gravity.

Prehistoric Forest was located on the Marblehead Peninsula, not far from Sandusky. Movie buffs who remember the 1995 film *Tommy Boy*, which was set in Sandusky, might recall the scene where Chris Farley and David Spade see a Prehistoric Forest park with a dinosaur by the sign. Visitors often thought the park in the movie was meant to be the attraction in Marblehead, park owner Len Tieman told the *Port Clinton News Herald* in 2010, the year the park closed.

"A lot of folks come in and want to get their picture by the gate because of the movie," Tieman told the newspaper. "It's a riot."

The ten-acre park opened in 1953 and continued to entertain generations of visitors who brought their children and grandchildren to the beloved attraction.

By the time Tieman and his wife bought the park in 1995, it was closed and up for sheriff's sale. Tieman was recovering from cancer, and his wife thought running the attraction would be a fun distraction, he told the newspaper.

The park was neglected, overgrown and filled with gray dinosaurs in dubious shape, so the Tiemans immediately got to work. Len fixed and painted some of the old dinosaurs and made new ones out of Styrofoam

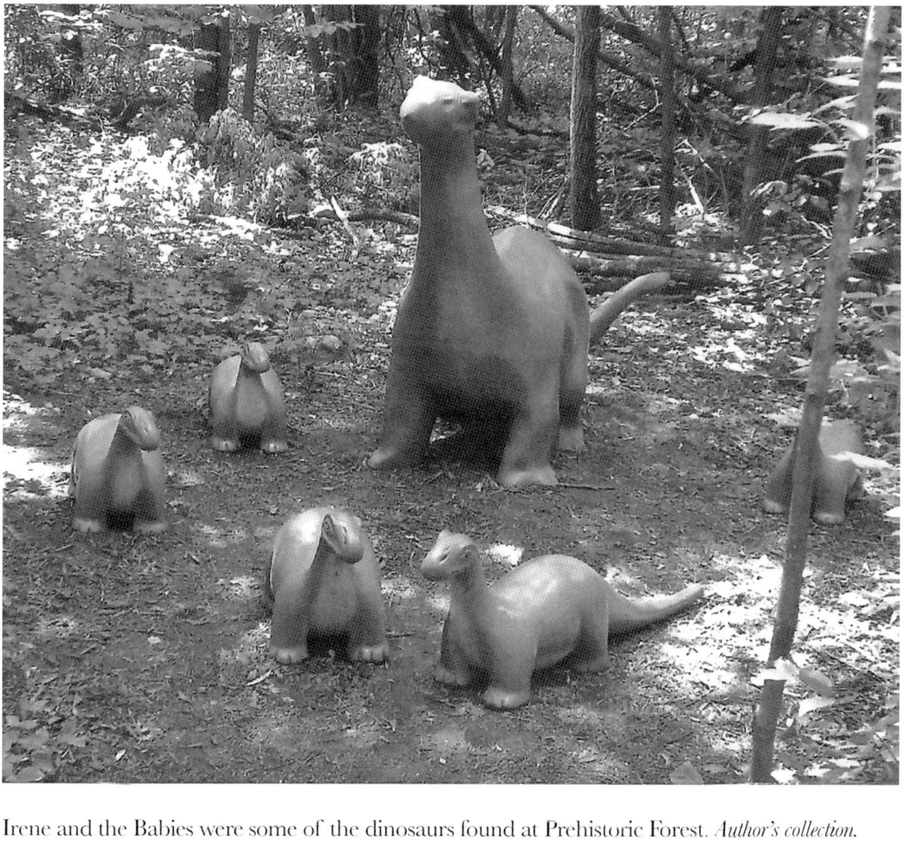

Irene and the Babies were some of the dinosaurs found at Prehistoric Forest. *Author's collection.*

covered with fiberglass. Most were brightly colored, and they included a sea dinosaur called a plesiosaurus, a brontosaurus and a small green dinosaur with its young, lovingly referred to as Irene and the Babies. When the park closed, it had about two dozen dinosaurs.

Mystery Hill was a favorite among older kids. Inside, water ran uphill because the cabin was built on an angle.

Thousands visited the park each year, but attendance began to decline as the popularity of video games and other children's amusements rose. So the Tiemans decided to make 2010 the park's last season.

Len told the *News Herald* that he planned to retire, and he and his wife wanted to enjoy the park's woods with its wildflowers and good spots to bird watch.

# BIBLIOGRAPHY

## Books


Butler, Margaret Manor. *A Pictorial History of the Western Reserve, 1796–1860*. Solon, OH: Early Settlers Association of the Western Reserve, 1963.

Christiansen, Harry. *Lake Shore Electric Railway*. Cleveland, OH: self-published, 1963.

Folwell, William Watts. *William Watts Folwell: The Autobiography and Letters of a Pioneer Culture*. Edited by Solon Buck. Minneapolis: University of Minnesota Press, 1933.

Francis, David W., and Diane DeMali Francis. *Cedar Point: Queen of American Watering Places*. Canton, OH: Daring Books, 1988.

Frohman, Charles. *Sandusky's Third Dimension*. Columbus: Ohio Historical Society, 1971.

Hansen, Helen. *At Home in Early Sandusky*. N.p., 1975.

Hill, Charles M., and William F. Bolly. *What: Souvenir of Sandusky, Ohio, and the Islands of Lake Erie*. Sandusky, OH: self-published, 1903.

Keeler, Lucy Elliot. *Old Fort Sandoski of 1745 and the Sandusky Country*. Columbus: Ohio Historical Society, 1908.

Koroknay, Tom. *Lyman Boats: Legend of the Lakes*. N.p.: self-published, 2004.

Kuebeler, Glenn C. *Castalia, Cold Creek, and the Blue Hole*. Charleston, SC: Arcadia Publishing, 2007.

Lake Erie Islands Historical Society. *Lake Erie Islands: Sketches and Stories of the First Century after the Battle of Lake Erie*. Edited by Michael Gora. Put-in-Bay, OH: Lake Erie Islands Historical Society, 2004.

# BIBLIOGRAPHY


Martin, Jessie A. *The Beginning and Tales of the Lake Erie Islands*. N.p.: self-published, 1990.

Musson, Robert A. *Brewing Beer in the Buckeye State*. Vol. 1. Medina, OH: Zepp Publications, 2013.

Peeke, Hewson L. *The Centennial History of Erie County, Ohio*. Vol. 1. Cleveland, OH: Penton Press, 1925.

———. *A Standard History of Erie County*. Vol. 1. Chicago: Lewis Publishing Company, 1916.

*Sandusky Area Sesquicentennial*. Sandusky, OH: Sandusky Area Sesquicentennial Inc., 1968.

Upton, Harriet Taylor. *History of the Western Reserve*. Vol. 1. Chicago: Lewis Publishing Company, 1910.

Wagner, Richard. *Golden Wheels: The Story of the Automobiles Made in Cleveland and Northeastern Ohio, 1892–1932*. Cleveland, OH: Western Reserve Historical Society, 1975.

Wendt, Gordon. *In the Wake of "Walk-in-the-Water."* Sandusky, OH: self-published, 1984.


## Interviews


Douglas Aden, Ohio Department of Natural Resources.

Rod Althaus, owner of New Wave Dive Shop in Port Clinton.

Bill Biehl of Sandusky.

Ron Davidson, Sandusky Library special collections librarian.

Bryan Edwards, Cedar Point public relations manager.

Bill Ehrnsberger, Sandusky City Schools brand development and retention and recruitment coordinator.

Jean Gardner of Sandusky.

Dina Heyman, Rieger Place Apartments.

Tom Koroknay of Lexington, Ohio.

Glenn C. Kuebeler, Castalia native.

Mike Marsinko of Sandusky.

Ken Miller, Cedar Point employee.

Paul Moon, president of the Ottawa County Historical Society.

Ray Niehm of Perkins Township.

Rich Norgard of Catawba Island.

Jim Norrocky of Crystal Rock.

# BIBLIOGRAPHY

Jeff Phillips of Lakeside.
Steve Sessler, Castalia Trout Club manager.
Barb Vanasco of Sandusky.
Ernie Washington of Catawba Island.

## Newspapers

*Cleveland Plain Dealer*
*Cleveland Press*
*Lakefront News*
*Lorain Morning Journal*
*News-Messenger* (Fremont)
*New York Clipper*
*Port Clinton Herald and Republican*
*Port Clinton News Herald*
*RFD News*
*Sandusky Register*, including a once regular feature called the "Follett House Scrapbook"
*Sandusky Star-Journal*
*Toledo Blade*

## Magazines

*Americana*
*Central Headlight*
*Cleveland Scene*
*Fire Lands Pioneer*
*Lighthouse Digest*
*Lookout*
*Motor Boating*
*New Yorker*
*Women's Endeavor*

# BIBLIOGRAPHY

## Other Publications

City of Sandusky business directories.
*Historical Society of Northwestern Ohio Quarterly Bulletin* (January 1937).
Lucas County/Maumee Valley Historical Society. *Ohio Cures* (May/June 1999, October 1999).
*Monthly Bulletin of Erie County Employment Service* (March 1966).
Owens-Illinois. Informational pamphlet, 1973.

## Public Records

Erie County Auditor's Office property records.

## Academic/Research Papers

American Crayon Company brochures.
Barr Rubber brochures.
Beattie, Homer M. "The Location of British Fort Sandusky." On file at the Ottawa County Historical Museum.
Edwards, Thomas J. "The Sandusky Forts." Ottawa County Historical Society, 1966. On file at the Ottawa County Historical Museum.
Frohman, Charles E. "Searching for the Forts and Indian Villages of Sandusky Bay." On file at the Rutherford B. Hayes Presidential Center.
Hinde and Dauch Paper Company history.
Laning, Paul F. "Sandusky Under Three Flags." On file at the Ottawa County Historical Museum.
"Location of the Sandusky Forts." On file at the Ottawa County Historical Museum.
M. Hommel Winery company history.
Sandusky Library Archives files.
Sandusky Tool Company history.

# BIBLIOGRAPHY

## Museum Exhibits

Lake Erie and Mad River and Nickel Plate Railroad Museum, Bellevue, Ohio.
Maritime Museum of Sandusky.
Town Hall Museum at Cedar Point.

## Websites

Detroit Historical Society. www.detroithistorical.org.
Johnson's Island Preservation Society. www.johnsonsisland.org.
Sandusky City Schools. www.sandusky-city.k12.oh.us.

# INDEX

# INDEX

# INDEX

## Z

# ABOUT THE AUTHOR

M. Kristina Smith has worked in newspapers for twelve years, working as a reporter and most recently as an assistant editor/reporter. She has worked for the *Port Clinton News Herald* and the Fremont *News-Messenger* since 2004. She is a graduate of Eastern Michigan University. This is her first book.

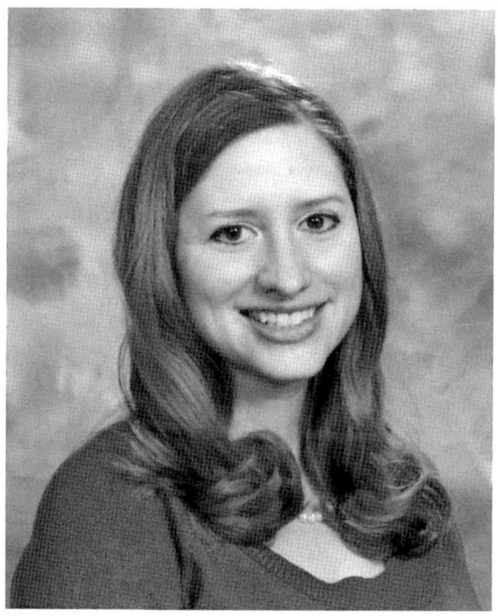